'The battle belonged that morning to the thin, wet line of khaki that dragged itself ashore on the channel coast of France'

General Omar M. Bradley

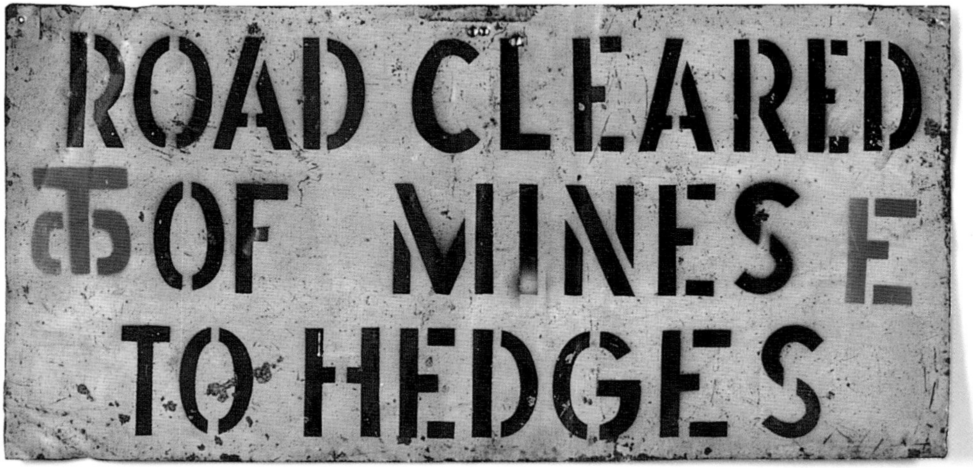
ROAD CLEARED
OF MINES E
TO HEDGES

THE
D-DAY KIT BAG
The Ultimate Guide to the Allied Assault on Europe

MARTIN ROBSON

CONWAY.

First published in Great Britain in 2014 by
Conway Publishing
A division of the Pavilion Books Group Ltd
10 Southcombe Street
London W14 0RA
www.conwaypublishing.com
Twitter: @conwaybooks

Distributed in the US and Canada by Sterling
Publishing Co. Ltd
387 Park Avenue South, New York, NY 100016-8810

British Library Cataloguing in Publication Data:
A catalogue record for this book is available from the British Library.

ISBN 978 1 84486 232 0

10 9 8 7 6 5 4 3 2 1

Edited with additional text and captions by Christopher Westhorp
Designed by Blok Graphic, London
Map artwork supplied by Barking Dog Art
Printed and bound by Toppan Leefung Printing Ltd, China

This book can be ordered direct from the publisher at
www.conwaypublishing.com

To receive regular email updates on forthcoming Conway titles, email info@
conwaypublishing.com with Conway Update in the subject field.

PICTURE CREDITS

Corbis 9, 42, 52, 64, 155; Conway Picture Library 2, 16, 23, 92, 94,
105, 130, 133; Getty Images 80, 118.

Commissioned colour photographs, including all uniforms, kit,
weapons and artefacts, are © Conway Picture Library/Pavilion
Books Group Archive.

ACKNOWLEDGEMENTS

I owe a debt of thanks to a number of people. Most importantly, my
friend and former colleague Dr Jon Robb-Webb of King's College
London's Defence Studies Department, who shares my obsessive
fascination with the events leading up to and following 6 June 1944.
His influence has shaped some of my thinking, especially with regard
to Operation NEPTUNE. Here I must also thank Dr Andrew Gordon
whose much anticipated forthcoming book on Admiral Bertram
Ramsay will more than fill a gap in the literature, providing an
unparalleled insight into the career and mind of NEPTUNE's driving
force. Dr David Hall has been a valuable sounding board for the Allied
and German air perspectives. Others who also take part in regular
discussions about Normandy and to whom I owe thanks include
Professor Greg Kennedy and Drs Harry Dickinson and Niall Barr. I
have had the pleasure of sharing many 'Staff Rides' to Normandy with
military staff and students of the Joint Services Command and Staff
College. Such trips promote much discussion of the events of D-Day
and in particular I would like to thank as Directors of Royal Naval
Division (RND), Cdr Kevin Fleming and Cdr John Cunningham, as well
as their Directing Staff: Cdr Dean Roberts, Lt-Cdrs Phil Coope, Tracy
Peyman, Zoe Briant-Evans and Lt-Cdrs (retd) Ed Sutcliffe and Alistair
Robertson, Maj Brian Usher (RM), Lt-Col Dan Rawlins (RDG), Sqn
Ldr Hedley Myers and Sqn Ldr Martin Cowie (RAF). At Anova Books
John Lee provides much encouragement, tinged with the realism that
academics sometimes require as to what can be achieved in such a
format, while Christopher Westhorp has been a meticulous editor. All
have contributed in some way to this book. Of course any errors that
remain are mine and mine alone.

My chosen profession of studying and writing about war is a
humbling experience – war is, after all, about human beings inflicting
violence, bloodshed and killing upon one another. The most poignant
accounts left behind by those who sacrificed their youth, and in many
cases their lives, in serving their respective causes, are the pained and
very moving references to the comfort and normality of home and
family. Many served and died so that successive generations can enjoy
such normality; for me the freedom of normality is to be found in time
spent with Charlotte, Horatio and Lysander.

Martin Robson, Ide, 28 November 2013

CONTENTS

PAGE ONE Between November 1943 and June 1944 the Germans had laid more than 4 million mines along, and inland from, the Normandy coastline, which meant that clearing paths to enable Allied infantry and vehicles to advance was a priority.

PAGE TWO The view from a Landing Craft Assault (LCA) as American infantrymen, struggling in the water because they are weighed down with heavy kit, begin their lengthy trek to the shore from the beached position of the LCA. The prone men visible ahead of them are either dead or seeking what cover they can from the withering storm of German machine gun fire from undamaged strongpoints.

PAGE THREE Weapons dropped for or made by the French Resistance. This group includes delayed-action explosives and incendiary devices. Of note are the incendiary matches and the home-made fragmentation grenade.

ABOVE General Patton's pistols. The Colt .45in single action revolver (top) has non-factory engraving and initialled ivory grips. The Smith and Wesson .357in Magnum revolver (bottom) also has initialled ivory grips and was sent to Patton in 1935.

INTRODUCTION

'You are about to embark upon the Great Crusade, toward which we have striven these many months. The eyes of the world are upon you. The hopes and prayers of liberty-loving people everywhere march with you. In company with our brave Allies and brothers-in-arms on other Fronts, you will bring about the destruction of the German war machine, the elimination of Nazi tyranny over the oppressed peoples of Europe, and security for ourselves in a free world.'

The words of General Dwight D. Eisenhower, Supreme Allied Commander of the Allied Expeditionary Force, reflect the importance of the Allied invasion of northwest Europe in June 1944. This entailed the largest amphibious assault ever launched. The plan called for a joint air, sea and land operation to land 175,000 men across the beaches or from the air by parachute and glider along 50 miles (80 kilometres) of the Normandy coastline. They would be supported by 3,000 artillery pieces, 1,500 tanks and 15,000 other vehicles. All would be landed on one day: D-Day.

Hitler's Atlantic Wall

The problem facing the forces of the United States, Britain, Canada and other countries from the British Commonwealth – as well as the Free French, Poles and Norwegians that made this a truly Allied operation – was how to crack Hitler's Atlantic Wall. This was less a wall and more a series of defensive positions that were constructed following a number of raids by Allied forces in 1942. Under the general concept of building a 'Fortress Europe', construction was the responsibility of the German labour force Organisation Todt and the wall itself was supposed to stretch from Norway to the Pyrenees, deterring any Allied landing along that coastline. Hitler was convinced that the fortifications would hold firm against any attempted invasion, forcing the Allies to withdraw from the European theatre of the war and thereby allow him to turn the tide of conflict in the east against the Soviet Union.

This is important, for the German defence of western Europe must be set against the wider context of a two-front war in which German materiel and manpower were being ground down by the brutal conflict on the

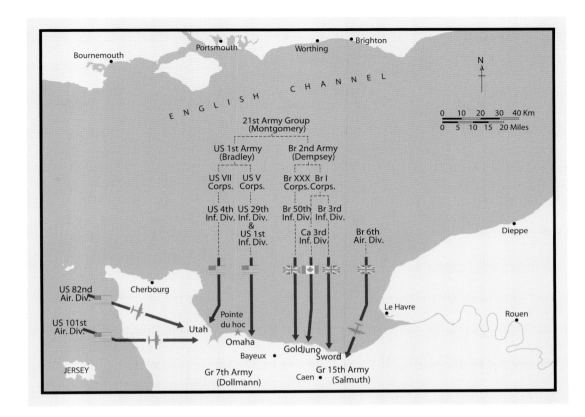

LEFT A contextual map of Operation OVERLORD, showing the key formations involved, the five Allied landing beaches and the airborne drops planned on the western and eastern flanks.

Eastern Front. In early 1944 the Germans had 179 divisions on the Eastern Front and a further 26 in southeast Europe, compared with 53 in France and the Low Countries, with a further 22 in Italy and 16 in Scandinavia. On 6 June 1944 only a further six divisions had been added to the defence of France and the Low Countries bringing the total up to 59, of which 20 were static defensive formations. As the Allies landed, there were still 165 German divisions fighting the Russians

and 28 in Italy. Importantly, however, of the Panzer divisions, while there were 18 in the east, 15 were now theoretically available for use against the Western allies.

Manning the Atlantic Wall in Normandy in June 1944 were the 709th Infantry Division on the east of the Cherbourg Peninsula, the 352nd Infantry Division on the Calvados coastline and the 716th Static Division around the River Orne and the city of Caen. The closest armoured formation was the 21st Panzer Division, elements of which were around Caen. Further to the southeast were the 12th SS Panzer 'Hitler Jugend' and the Panzer Lehr divisions, with the 2nd SS Panzer Division 'Das Reich' in southwestern France. If an Allied invasion were to be defeated, the Panzer formations would be crucial.

There remained the problem of how to use them most effectively. There was disagreement among German commanders over both the 'Fortress Europe' concept and how to defend the west. Most believed an Allied landing would strike at the Pas-de-Calais, the shortest crossing for an invasion force, and German priorities had been focused there. A further consideration was the location for the V1 and V2 missiles with which Hitler hoped to terrorise Britain into accepting German dominance of western Europe. Once the coastline of Scandinavia was factored in, along with positions in Italy and the Mediterranean, Hitler's defence concept of not abandoning conquests led to an attempt to defend everything and a consequent inability to concentrate German forces. With Allied attacks in the Mediterranean and the German focus on the Eastern Front, it was only in November 1943 that – following concerns voiced by the German commander in the west Field Marshal Gerd von Rundstedt – Hitler started to strengthen western defences as an Allied invasion seemed likely for 1944. Following this, Hitler appointed Field Marshal Erwin Rommel to command Army Group B, tasked with the defence of the Atlantic Coast.

Rommel's appointment highlighted the fundamental problem of command responsibility. Rommel was in command of the defence of the coastline but the Panzer formations were the responsibility of General Leo Freiherr Geyr von Schweppenburg who commanded Panzer Group West. Geyr von Schweppenburg, drawing on the examples of Allied landings at Sicily and Anzio, was concerned about the effect Allied naval gunfire would have on armoured formations near the coast and argued they should be concentrated further inland. Rommel, who in North Africa had witnessed first-hand the effect that Allied airpower could have on armoured units, was convinced that the Allies must be defeated at the beaches and he wanted a concentration of effort there, including the deployment of Panzer formations.

The failure to agree a coherent strategy went all the way to the top. In March 1944, Hitler gave Rommel three Panzer divisions, left three with Rundstedt and kept four under central German Army control. Such a disjointed operational command was also reflected in air defence, including *Fallschirmjäger* (paratroopers) and flak batteries, which were under the separate command of Field Marshal Hugo Sperrle as part of *Luftflotte* 3. The *Kriegsmarine*'s Navy Group West, under Admiral Krancke, was responsible for the positioning of naval guns and as such they were located to meet naval

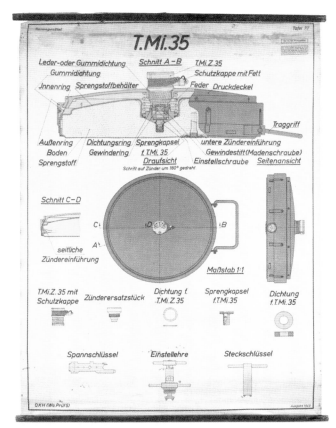

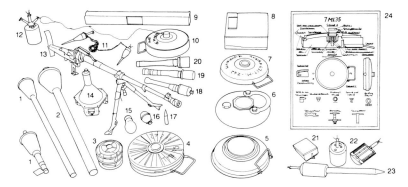

GERMAN ANTI-TANK AND ANTI-PERSONNEL WEAPONS

1 Panzerfaust 1
2 Panzerfaust 60
3 Glasmine 43
4 Teller mine 35 (steel)
5 Teller mine 42 (mushroom) anti-tank
6 Topf mine (non-magnetic, bottom view)
7 Teller mine 42
8 Wood box for mine 42
9 Riegel bar mine 43
10 Teller smoke mine 35 Fumigene
11 Pull and pressure ignition detonators
12 S mine 'bouncing betty' anti-personnel
13 Panzerbuchse 38, 7.92mm anti-armour
14 Anti-tank shaped charge (magnetic, 3kg)
15 Blenkorper 2H glass smoke grenade
16 M1939 hand grenade
17 Round (7.92mm) for Panzerbuchse 38
18 M1943 stick grenade
19 M1924 smoke grenade
20 M1924 stick fragmentation grenade
21 Anti-personnel wooden 'shoe' mine 42
22 S mine with interior
23 Anti-personnel mine
24 Army training chart for Teller mine 35

needs, not necessarily to defend against an amphibious assault. Clearly, in terms of command structures, the German defence of the west was at best disjointed and at worst divisive, based upon compromise between

Franz Gockel

3rd *Kompanie*, 726th Infantry Regiment, *Widerstandnest* 62, Colleville-sur-Mer, OMAHA beach

· ·

In February, 1944, during his inspection of the defences of the Normandy coast, Field Marshal Rommel had visited our position. He had sharply criticised not only the lack of defences constructed at our position but also those along the entire coastline from Colleville-sur-Mer to Vierville-sur-Mer. He compared the bay in our sector with the bay at Salerno in Italy and urgently ordered further defences to be constructed.

During the several weeks preceding June 6, two casemates for 75mm guns were poured and only the steel aperture covers were lacking. The openings in the apertures were the size of a barn door and offered a perfect target for the attackers. Our bunker, with its more than two-metre-thick concrete ceiling, had also been completed in May.

We constructed tank barriers on the beach at low tide from logs topped with Teller mines. Other beach obstacles were 'Czech hedgehogs' made from crossed iron beams, and 'Belgian gates' from thick steel stakes.

competing personalities rather than being a synergy of land, sea and air assets.

Nowhere was this more evident than the German inability to use air assets to attack the Allied invasion flotilla as it assembled in ports and harbours along the south coast of England. In trying to provide some air support on D-Day itself, the *Luftwaffe* could only mount 319 sorties. Furthermore, apart from very rare occasions, such as the attack by German E-boats on Operation TIGER off Slapton Sands in April 1944 in which over 900 American servicemen lost their lives, German naval assets could not interdict the invasion once it was launched. Fundamentally, due to Allied degradation of the *Luftwaffe* and the *Kriegsmarine* the Germans could only really defend the Atlantic coast *at* the coast and inland, rather than at a distance. So, for Rommel and the men of the 352nd Infantry and 716th Static divisions, it was a waiting game in which every passing day allowed them to strengthen their defences.

At every level, strategic, operational and tactical, the Germans lacked sufficient manpower to mount a fulsome defence. The formations assigned to the west were a mixed bag. The best were the SS Panzer formations, with the 12th SS Panzer comprising over 21,000 young, ideologically driven Nazi fanatics. But the troops assigned to the coastline were a different matter. Many formations were seriously understrength, with their best men already transferred to the east. The motivation of those who remained was suspect; some were older men enjoying a comfortable posting to the

French coast, others were very young, such as Franz Gockel who had just celebrated his 18th birthday, and lacked training and combat experience. In fact, many troops spent the weeks before D-Day building defences rather than training. There was a degree of complacency among many German men, officers and NCOs. Compounding these issues, reinforcements to these units were often *Osttruppen* volunteers and conscripts drawn from the German-occupied territories in the east, such as Poles, Czechs, Romanians and those from the Soviet Asiatic territories, along with troops recruited from Soviet prisoners of war (POWs). While estimates for the number of *Osttruppen* varies from 1:5 to 1:6 of all "German" troops in Normandy, what is crucial is that there was a significant number of non-Germans manning the coastal defences, including the 441st Ost Battalion, tasked with holding up the Allied invasion until the Panzers could react. Finally, the infantry units were fundamentally static formations – immobile, lacking logistic support and, in the view of General Major Speidel, Rommel's Chief of Staff, very much akin to a First World War division.

The polyglot nature of the German defenders was reflected in their equipment, which included captured French, Polish, Czech and Russian mortars and guns. Within this international collection there were variations in calibre (and hence ammunition requirements), creating a logistical nightmare. Given their strategic, operational and logistic problems, the Germans were still extremely skilled at utilising the terrain to create strong tactical defensive positions. Obstacles were planted up to the high-water mark on the beaches, including mined posts, mined 'Belgian Gates' at the low-water mark and 'Czech hedgehogs' (huge metal caltrops). All were designed to punch a hole in the hull of landing craft. Central to the defence of the beaches was the concept of *Widerstandnest*, or 'Resistance Nests', a cluster of mutually supporting positions based around bunkers and pillboxes containing anti-tank weapons (including the formidable 88mm) placed in enfilade firing positions, heavy machine guns such as the MG42, rifle pits, mortar pits, infantry trenches, sniper positions, minefields and barbed wire. These were sited to cover the exits from the beaches and provided interlocking fields of fire.

Rommel reinvigorated the existing defences along the Normandy and Brittany coastlines. Between his appointment, in November 1943, and May 1944, German forces laid over four million mines and constructed over half a million obstacles. These included the famous 'Rommel's Asparagus' designed to stop glider landings. Concrete was used to casemate guns and build new bunkers, foxholes and anti-tank ditches were dug, and extra beach obstacles were constructed. Some of these improvements were complete, with many more still in progress, by the summer of 1944. Any attacker was presented with a range of challenges by the German defences, whose main object was to hold up the invasion while the mobile Panzer reserves came up to throw the Allies back into the sea.

BELOW The English-made Gestetner duplicator that was used at Allied Supreme Headquarters to print Eisenhower's original one-page message (right), which was later issued to all the invasion participants.

SUPREME HEADQUARTERS
ALLIED EXPEDITIONARY FORCE

Soldiers, Sailors and Airmen of the Allied Expeditionary Force!

You are about to embark upon the Great Crusade, toward which we have striven these many months. The eyes of the world are upon you. The hopes and prayers of liberty-loving people everywhere march with you. In company with our brave Allies and brothers-in-arms on other Fronts, you will bring about the destruction of the German war machine, the elimination of Nazi tyranny over the oppressed peoples of Europe, and security for ourselves in a free world.

Your task will not be an easy one. Your enemy is well trained, well equipped and battle-hardened. He will fight savagely.

But this is the year 1944! Much has happened since the Nazi triumphs of 1940-41. The United Nations have inflicted upon the Germans great defeats, in open battle, man-to-man. Our air offensive has seriously reduced their strength in the air and their capacity to wage war on the ground. Our Home Fronts have given us an overwhelming superiority in weapons and munitions of war, and placed at our disposal great reserves of trained fighting men. The tide has turned! The free men of the world are marching together to Victory!

I have full confidence in your courage, devotion to duty and skill in battle. We will accept nothing less than full Victory!

Good Luck! And let us all beseech the blessing of Almighty God upon this great and noble undertaking.

Dwight D Eisenhower

RIGHT Just prior to the invasion, Eisenhower wrote this draft announcement to be made in the event that the landings failed. The incorrect date (July 5) indicates the stress that the Supreme Commander and his staff at SHAEF HQ must have felt at the time.

BELOW The personal message from General Montgomery that was read out to all the troops of the 21st Army Group before D-Day.

21 ARMY GROUP

PERSONAL MESSAGE FROM THE C-in-C

To be read out to all Troops

1. The time has come to deal the enemy a terrific blow in Western Europe.

The blow will be struck by the combined sea, land, and air forces of the Allies—together constituting one great Allied team, under the supreme command of General Eisenhower.

2. On the eve of this great adventure I send my best wishes to every soldier in the Allied team.

To us is given the honour of striking a blow for freedom which will live in history; and in the better days that lie ahead men will speak with pride of our doings. We have a great and a righteous cause.

Let us pray that " The Lord Mighty in Battle " will go forth with our armies, and that His special providence will aid us in the struggle.

3. I want every soldier to know that I have complete confidence in the successful outcome of the operations that we are now about to begin.

With stout hearts, and with enthusiasm for the contest, let us go forward to victory.

4. And, as we enter the battle, let us recall the words of a famous soldier spoken many years ago :—

" He either fears his fate too much,
Or his deserts are small,
Who dare not put it to the touch,
To win or lose it all."

5. Good luck to each one of you. And good hunting on the mainland of Europe.

B. L. Montgomery
General
C-in-C 21 Army Group.

1944.

Our landings in the Cherbourg – Havre area have failed to gain a satisfactory foothold and I have withdrawn the troops. (withdrawn.) This particular operation my decision to attack at this time and place was based upon the best information available. The troops, the air and the Navy did all that Bravery and devotion to duty could do. If any blame or fault attaches to the attempt it is mine alone.

July 5

Origins of OVERLORD

As soon as the dust had settled from the Dunkirk evacuation in 1940, most British strategists understood that defeating Germany would entail an invasion of Europe. When the United States of America (USA) entered the conflict, in December 1941, the main priority for Britain's prime minister Winston Churchill was to convince the Americans to defeat Germany first, before turning to Japan.

With Churchill's aim achieved, planning for the invasion of Europe began at the ARCADIA Conference, held in Washington, DC, between 22 December 1941 and 14 January 1942. The conference scoped out the need for fully integrated Allied planning and command structures under the auspices of the Supreme Headquarters Allied Expeditionary Force (SHAEF). With this agreed, in early 1942 Allied planners began to think about how to conduct a cross-Channel invasion, codenamed Operation SLEDGEHAMMER. It also had to be set against the context of Allied operations in North Africa and the Mediterranean, as discussed at the Casablanca Conference in early 1943.

But launching a full-blown Allied invasion from the UK was dependent upon the build-up of men, materiel and supplies, a process called Operation BOLERO. That in turn involved ensuring that Atlantic sea lines of communication remained relatively secure, for despite some successes the German U-boat campaign against Allied shipping was not a sustained threat thanks to the convoy system. Further work on the invasion plan continued, culminating in early 1943 when Lieutenant General Frederick Morgan was appointed Chief of Staff to the Supreme Allied Commander (COSSAC). Told by Field Marshal Lord Alanbrooke that 'It won't work, but you must bloody well make it', Morgan found himself a room in Norfolk House, London, and started planning for the largest amphibious invasion in history. Morgan's appointment was crucial, providing focus and clarity to the plan. He spent much of 1943 producing a detailed study and many of the problems associated with the plan were discussed in late June at the conference codenamed RATTLE held at Lord Mountbatten's Combined Operations training centre in Scotland, which was also attended by American and Canadian planners. With the Pas-de-Calais and Normandy identified as the only two possible invasion sites, at RATTLE – given the formidable German defences in the Pas-de-Calais – Normandy was selected as the location for the operation now named OVERLORD. It would consist of a three-division amphibious assault at beaches codenamed OMAHA, GOLD and JUNO and a one-division airborne drop. D-Day was set as May 1944.

'It won't work, but you must bloody well make it.'

Field Marshal Lord Alanbrooke, the British Chief of the imperial General Staff

The object of OVERLORD, as defined by Morgan on 30 July 1943, was not just an assault but 'to secure a lodgement area on the continent from which further offensive operations can be developed'. At the Quebec Conference in August 1943 British planners insisted that three criteria were met before OVERLORD could be launched: the reduction of the *Luftwaffe*; keeping the Germans occupied in Italy and elsewhere while Allied airpower attacked transport and supply routes into and within France in order to limit the units which could deploy against the invasion; and solving the problem of supplying the invasion forces across beaches.

These plans were formalised at Tehran in November 1943 when Churchill, Roosevelt and Stalin met to discuss the COSSAC plan. With Stalin accusing Churchill of being reluctant to invade, Churchill restated his belief in the plan – but only once the three conditions had been met. The Western allies were committed to an invasion of northwest Europe and Churchill wanted to launch OVERLORD as much as anyone else did, but his view was that the timing had to be right. An amphibious invasion of France could not just be cobbled together and, in light of the catastrophic losses of British manpower during the First World War, Churchill was extremely concerned about the effect that large casualties might have on Britain's ability and appetite to continue the war, when compared with the superior manpower resources of the USA and Soviet Union.

With the plan agreed upon, key command appointments were made – none of them more important than the Supreme Commander Allied Forces General Dwight Eisenhower, who was appointed on 6 December 1943. Air Chief Marshal Sir Arthur Tedder was his deputy commander and Lieutenant General Beddell Smith replaced Morgan as his Chief of Staff. Morgan became Deputy Chief of Staff. COSSAC was incorporated into Eisenhower's command structure, Supreme Headquarters, Allied Expeditionary Force (SHAEF). All of the component commanders under Eisenhower were British: General Sir Bernard Montgomery as Commander of the Allied 21st Army Group, Air Chief Marshal Sir Trafford Leigh-Mallory as Allied Expeditionary Air Force Commander and Admiral Sir Bertram Ramsay as Allied Naval Commander. One of Eisenhower's main priorities was managing the inevitable frictions between such strong personalities.

With key commanders in position, Morgan's July 1943 plan was revised with Montgomery and his staff at 21st Army Group assuming much of the planning, except for the naval parts which he wisely left to Ramsay (the two had worked together well during the Allied invasion of Sicily in 1943). The major change was widening the initial assault to include the flank beaches of UTAH

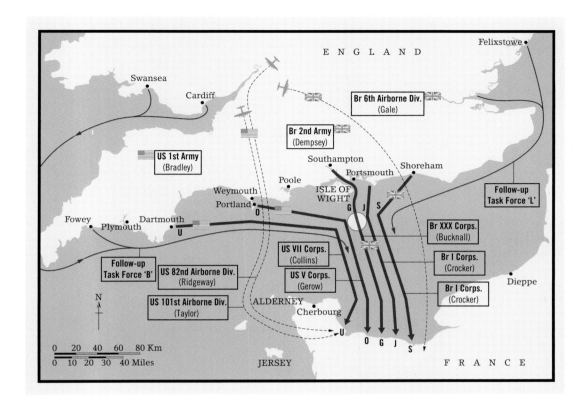

Force U (Utah) = 12 convoys
Force O (Omaha) = 9 convoys
Force G (Gold) = 16 convoys
Force J (Juno) = 10 convoys
Force S (Sword) = 12 convoys
Piccadilly Circus

LEFT The Allied air and naval invasion routes of Operation OVERLORD. To prevent any losses to friendly anti-aircraft fire the airborne transit routes stayed clear of the naval transit routes.

to the west, closer to the key port of Cherbourg, and SWORD to the east, where the River Orne and Canal provided a barrier to any German counter-attack. This enabled the Allies to land more men on D-Day but it required a greater logistical effort; for example, a shortage of landing craft was an acute problem, leading to an inevitable delay. The widened plan also required airborne landings to secure the beach exits at UTAH and to seize and hold key positions on the British flank.

Given the importance of weather conditions in the Channel, and taking into account the moon phase and the tides, 5 June 1944 was identified as the new D-Day.

SOE and the French Resistance
Gaining intelligence about German preparations and dispositions of units was an important part of Allied planning. This, and disrupting German movement and formations, was the work of the French Resistance

BELOW Weapons for silent killing supplied by the OSS and SOE. Clockwise, from the left: Liberator .45in single shot smoothbore pistol, with case, instructions and wooden ejector rod; Welrod 9mm single shot silenced pistol; High Standard Model H-D .22in semi-automatic pistol; and the High Standard Model B .22in semi-automatic pistol.

RIGHT British-made Resistance 'case' radio. This S-type portable radio was dropped onto Epaney, Normandy, on the night of 17 September 1943 and was just one of many different types of suitcase radio designed for clandestine broadcast and receipt of radio communications by the French Resistance and Allied agents.

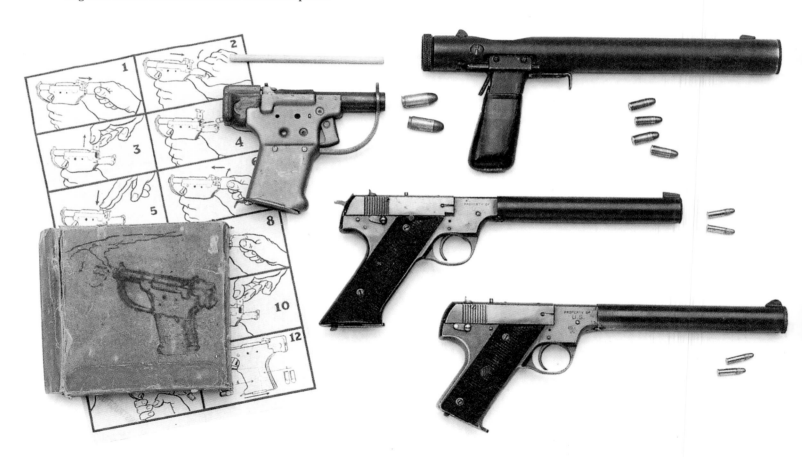

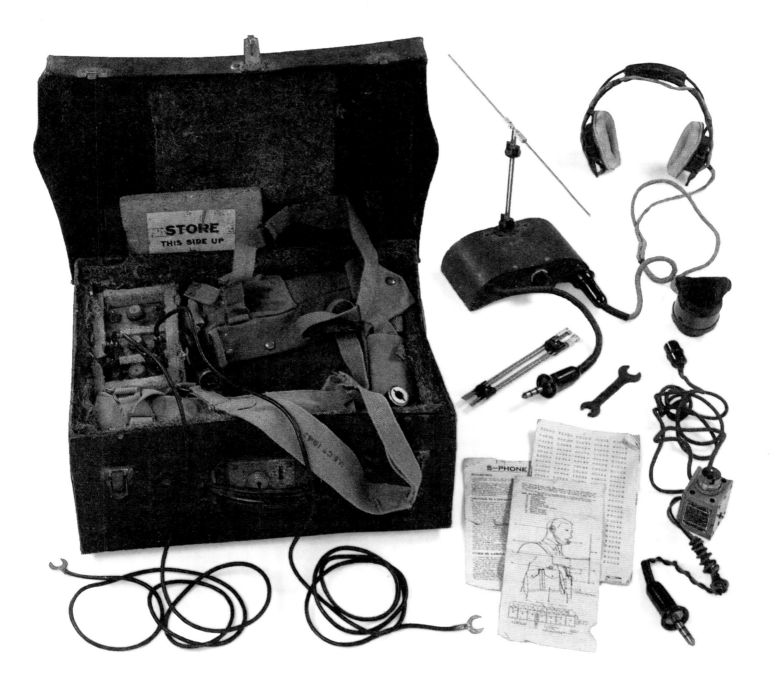

Monsieur La Navez

... on the evening of June 5, I heard the message: 'The call of the ploughman in the misty morning'.

• •

Everyone was pleased with the news, as on the radio we heard confirmation of the call. Five of us went to Grimbosq to blow up the railroad track. It was not far from the station, and in the long curve right before it, we blew up a length of about five or six carriages.

and teams of British operatives working as part of the Special Operations Executive (SOE). The romance of the partisan struggling against occupation is not wholly accurate; the Resistance was heavily splintered and often disorganised, rife with political intrigue. In early 1944 the SOE estimated the total number involved at 350,000, though those able to play an active combat role in supporting the invasion was considerably less than that. French railway workers were particularly important, providing information on troop movements and having the knowledge and opportunity for sabotage that would force German armour onto the road network. Other targets included communications, such as telephone cables or power lines. Resistance groups also provided vital intelligence about the German defences, such as the locations of minefields.

Three-man Jedburgh teams – consisting of a British SOE officer, an American from the OSS (Office of Strategic Services) and a French national from the Free French Intelligence and Operations Central Bureau – would be parachuted, in military uniform, into occupied France to train groups in the dark arts of sabotage. The first team did not, however, land until the night before D-Day. Free French parachutists of the British SAS Brigade would be dropped on the evening before D-Day as part of Operation TITANIC, a wider use of the SAS to cause havoc behind the enemy beaches. The evening before D-Day would see wirelesses messages sent to the French Resistance to commence the work of destruction in support of OVERLORD.

The OVERLORD plan

OVERLORD comprised four main phases: FORTITUDE, POINTBLANK, NEPTUNE and MULBERRY.

FORTITUDE: Operation FORTITUDE, eventually comprised FORTITUDE NORTH and SOUTH. This was the deception plan relating to the time and location of the invasion. Clearly the Germans were not so foolish as to ignore the possibilities of any landings in France, so Allied deception centred on where and when these would take place. FORTITUDE NORTH played on Hitler's much-vaunted obsession with Scandinavia

RIGHT The bombing of Pointe du Hoc in May 1944 was a vital part of the pre-invasion preparations at Omaha. The German battery had a commanding location overlooking the English Channel.

to tie down German troops in Norway to such effect that Hitler actually reinforced his positions there. FORTITUDE SOUTH was designed to convince Hitler that the invasion would occur at the Pas-de-Calais. This included stationing the Allies' most flamboyant general, and the one the Germans expected to lead the invasion, George S. Patton, in Kent at the head of the imaginary First United States Army Group (FUSAG), complete with 'dummy' tanks. With massive preparations along the entire south coast of England, the object was to convince the Germans that any landing in Normandy was a feint before the main landing, led by Patton, in the Pas-de-Calais. The Allies also played on German fears of a landing in the South of France to provide further distortion from the main effort.

To feed the Germans with precisely the right, seemingly credible, information to fool them, a complex web of spies and double agents run by the Double Cross (XX) Committee had been building a fake picture of Allied intentions. The Germans particularly trusted agents BRUTUS (real name Roman Czerniawski) and GARBO (Juan Pujol García). Their elaborate deceptions were added to fake radio transmissions from FUSAG. FORTITUDE also benefitted from the fact that the Allies, by cracking the German Enigma codes, could read enemy communications and used the knowledge gleaned to add realistic depth to their deception. The work of the French Resistance in cutting communication cables had a knock-on effect, pushing more German traffic towards radio and Enigma, which the Allies could intercept and decode. The *Luftwaffe* had been subjected to such a campaign of attrition by Allied air forces that it was unable to mount sustained reconnaissance flights over southern England. The deception worked to such an extent that on 5 June 1944 von Rundstedt was writing that the Allied attack was not imminent and when it did come the main landing would be at the Pas-de-Calais. For his 'work' in June 1944 the Germans awarded GARBO an Iron Cross; he was later awarded an MBE for his real work for MI5.

POINTBLANK: Securing air superiority was a vital prerequisite to launching the invasion. Commencing

Robert Slaughter
Company D, 116th Regimental Combat Team, 29th Division

• •

We embarked on the Cunard line's luxury liner, HMS [sic] Queen Mary, the most modern and fastest luxury liner afloat. It was converted to a troopship, stripped of its luxury, and painted dull gray. Hammocks were installed and with the troops sleeping in shifts, there was room for approximately 25,000 troops and crew.

On 27 September [1943] we said good-bye to the Statue of Liberty and set sail for the British Isles. Since this was a British liner, we were fed British food, which was absolutely awful.

in June 1943, the second necessary phase identified in the OVERLORD plan was Operation POINTBLANK, the Allied strategic air assault to further downgrade the *Luftwaffe*, particularly by attacking German oil production and manufacturing, especially the ball bearing industry. This caused some friction with the 'Bomber Barons', such as Air Chief Marshal Arthur Harris at the RAF's Bomber Command and General Carl Spaatz of the 8th USAAF, who both believed that the Allied strategic bombing campaign – to destroy German cities, manufacturing and the will of the German people – would bring the Nazi regime to its knees, thereby removing the need for a cross-Channel invasion at all. Hence, it was their intent to delay assigning forces to POINTBLANK until as late as possible. It was not until early 1944 that this became the case, and by April SHAEF had decided to use the final few months of the air campaign before the landing to attain two objects: the first was to destroy the remaining German fighter forces and their supporting industry to the point where they could not interfere with the invasion; the second was to attack enemy rail communications with Normandy. Given the distribution of German forces, it was essential to prevent them using their interior lines of communication, based mainly on rail transport, for moving troops from the South of France, the Mediterranean, Scandinavia and even the Eastern Front. In order to maintain the main tenet of FORTITUDE SOUTH: for every ton of bombs dropped on Normandy, two tons fell on the Pas-de-Calais.

ABOVE Insignia of three American infantry divisions, left to right: 1st (nicknamed 'The Big Red One'), 2nd ('Indianhead') and 4th ('Ivy').

For D-Day itself the Allied air forces operated to achieve six main tasks, the most crucial of which was protection of the huge armada as it left the ports and harbours of southern England for the Normandy coast. OVERLORD was not just an assault but a sustained invasion, which required ongoing logistical support. Allied air forces would continue to secure the airspace above the hundreds of ships carrying men, munitions and kit over to France and then returning with the wounded. The second task was to attack German beach and coastal defences, while the third was to provide air cover for the beaches themselves. Task four was interdicting enemy control and communications, while five was to provide the air part of the airborne landings. Task six was direct support of the land forces.

Subsidiary operations, in the forms of GLIMMER and TAXABLE, were designed to keep the Germans guessing as to the location of the real invasion. Operation GLIMMER produced a fake invasion of the

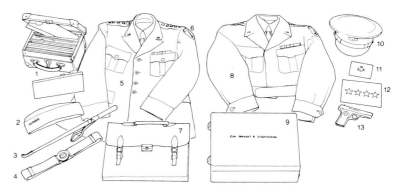

UNIFORMS AND MEMORABILIA OF GENERAL DWIGHT D. EISENHOWER

1 Leather map case containing linen-mounted maps of northwest Europe

2 General's garrison cap with four-star insignia (the rank Eisenhower was promoted to in February 1943 during the Tunisia campaign)

3 Leather riding crop with a silver band inscribed: 'General D.D. Eisenhower, Supreme Allied Commander, E.T.O. [European Theatre of Operations] 1944.'

4 General's pistol belt

5 General's summer service jacket with cotton khaki shirt and olive drab wool tie

6 SHAEF shoulder patch

7 Leather briefcase with interior marked 'Eisenhower, United States Army'

8 Field jacket, known as the 'Ike jacket', with four stars and SHAEF insignia

9 Dispatch case used by Eisenhower and staff at SHAEF

10 Officer's service cap with general's insignia

11 Cartier silver cigarette case, bearing the Great Seal of the United States, with a gold-washed interior engraved: 'To victorious General Ike Eisenhower, Xmas 1943, Selma and Maxine.'

12 Car pennant

13 Colt M380 auto pistol, SN135171, carried by General Eisenhower

ABOVE Insignia of the British 6th Airborne Division (with its winged Pegasus shoulder emblem) and the Combined Operations Command.

Pas-de-Calais. TAXABLE consisted of naval forces emitting radio traffic from a fake invasion force heading for a point further east on the Normandy coast while the Lancaster Bombers of 617 'Dambusters' Squadron dropped bundles of aluminium chaff called 'Window' to create a picture on German radar that resembled an invasion flotilla at sea. A British airborne raid, Operation BITING, in February 1942 had captured important equipment from a German Würzburg radar array near Bruneval. This had yielded information about German radar and what was necessary to fool it.

To achieve all the tasks required, the Allies assembled more than 10,000 aircraft. These were flown in more than 195,000 sorties in the weeks before D-Day, during which 12,000 Allied airmen were lost before the great naval armada even left port. The effect on the *Luftwaffe* was devastating; it lost over 5,500 aircraft in just three months between January and March 1944. More serious still, the Allied air campaign was killing more *Luftwaffe* pilots than could be replaced. On 6 June itself the *Luftwaffe* was more of an irritant to the Allied landings than a serious threat. Many Allied troops in the landings remarked that they did not see an enemy aircraft all day and the *Luftwaffe* only managed 319 sorties on D-Day. The full extent of Allied air supremacy over the south of England, the Channel and Normandy is revealed when that meagre total is compared to the 13,688 sorties flown by Allied air forces on D-Day – their aircraft displaying the distinctive black-and-white invasion stripes to prevent the 'blue on blue' incidents that had occurred during the Sicily landings. Of the overwhelming effect of Allied airpower, Franklin Roosevelt wryly noted that 'when Hitler built walls around his Fortress Europe he forgot to put a roof on it'.

NEPTUNE: The third, and absolutely crucial phase of the OVERLORD plan, was Operation NEPTUNE, the actual amphibious assault. Detailed planning for NEPTUNE was the responsibility of Admiral Sir Bertram Ramsay, who had overseen the evacuation of Dunkirk in 1940 and knew the English Channel very well. Ramsay was also an expert in amphibious operations, for he had been responsible for planning and implementing the Allied landings in North Africa in 1942 and Sicily in 1943. The broad outline of the plan called for arrangements to be made for getting men and material across the beaches; this would render the seizing of a port unnecessary. The assault would be

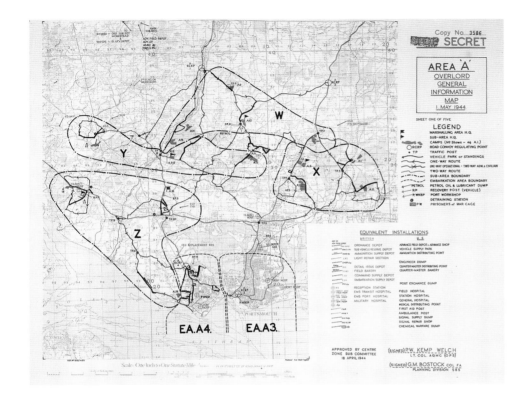

LEFT An original Top Secret administrative map of the Southampton and Portsmouth areas during the build-up to D-Day detailing the depots, hospitals, two-way routes, embarkation areas and much more.

launched at the weakest spot on the enemy coast that could be covered by the Allies' air and naval assets. In order to win the race for the beaches and prevent the invasion being thrown back into the sea by German reserves, the initial assault and the build-up of forces following that would have to be of sufficient strength to withstand German counter-attacks. In support of this aim, the French Resistance, SOE, air interdiction and naval gunfire would restrict enemy movement within and into the landing areas. Finally, through the continuance of FORTITUDE, it was essential to keep the Germans asking a crucial question: was this the actual invasion or just a feint for an Allied landing elsewhere? Fundamentally, the NEPTUNE plan called for an attack with 'maximum force and with the greatest attainable violence'.

Before the landing force could set sail, shaping operations had already been tipping the balance in

BELOW A selection of the original technical plans for the MULBERRY harbours, including the PHOENIX caisson breakwaters, concrete floats for the WHALE pier roadways and construction plans for pontoon units.

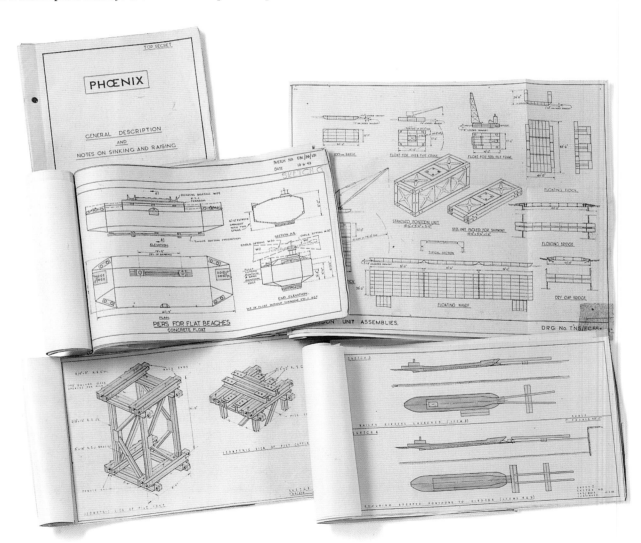

RIGHT A German Enigma enciphering machine. Building on pre-war work by the Poles, British mathematicians and cryptanalysts at Bletchley Park broke the Enigma machine's codes and were able to use German radio traffic to create an accurate picture of troop dispositions in Normandy.

favour of the Allies. Of course, in the Atlantic there was the U-boat menace to defeat, a victory achieved by late 1943/early 1944, and by the time of D-Day 2 million tons a month were entering UK ports. Direct naval shaping operations included the crippling of the German pocket battleship *Tirpitz* by carrier-borne aircraft in April 1944, thereby ensuring no German major surface ships would interfere with NEPTUNE. Combined Operations Pilotage Parties in their midget submarines, Motor Gun Boats and *folbot* canoes had all been busy surveying beaches right under the noses of the Germans.

For the invasion itself, the Allied Naval Expeditionary Force was divided into two Naval Task Forces: the Western under Rear-Admiral Alan G. Kirk (US Navy) and the Eastern under Rear-Admiral Sir Philip Vian (Royal Navy). With ships leaving numerous harbours along the south coast of England, the rendezvous point for the invasion was Area Z, to the southeast of the Isle of Wight and known more commonly as Piccadilly Circus. Here the invasion flotilla would gather and organise into the correct order of sailing for the respective Task Forces, each designated by a letter related to their beach – for instance, Task Force J would land at JUNO. The role of the larger warships was to provide cover and escort the flotilla of landing vessels and transports. Destroyers provided screens to each flank while anti-submarine patrols in the Western Approaches to the Channel negated the U-boat threat from the French Atlantic ports (as well as the danger posed by German fast E-boats or S-boats).

Each force would be accompanied by minesweepers, which would undertake the hazardous job of clearing ten channels through the German minefields to allow the flotilla secure passage to the Normandy coastline. Off SWORD, a largely featureless beach, the midget submarines *X20* and *X23* would be placed in advance to act as navigation buoys and guide the landing craft in. Capital ships would provide naval gunfire support (NGS) and vital logistical support to the waves of assault craft.

There were 2,486 landing craft with a variety of roles to fulfil. Some would drop special Duplex Drive (DD) swimming tanks to lead the beach assault. Landing Craft Assault (LCA) would carry the first wave of infantry. LCAs were carried on the davits of larger vessels, Landing Ship Infantry (LSI); about seven miles off the invasion beaches the LCAs were lowered and the infantry embarked into them (no easy task in poor weather and a heavy swell) for the final run in to the shore. One of the reasons for the delay in the invasion, from May to June 1944 after the addition of UTAH and SWORD beaches, was the Allies' shortage of landing craft. On D-Day itself the craft were to deliver their load of men and material to the beach, kedge off (one of the reasons for landing on a rising tide) and return to take in the next wave. The object was to have a continuous flow of troops and equipment landing on the beach to overwhelm the German defences. Apart from the LCA there were 45 other types of landing craft. Some were equipped with rockets, with which to saturate enemy positions, while the LCA(HR) was equipped with a Hedgehog spigot mortar firing 24 bombs that would, it was hoped, clear minefields and destroy obstacles. Others were designed to lay smoke barrages, or to carry anti-aircraft guns, while the Landing Craft Kitchens were necessary to sustain the naval personnel engaged in what would be a lengthy operation.

Ramsay's team was faced with bringing order to what was likely to be a complex and potentially chaotic situation. Key to the implementation of the NEPTUNE plan, and hence OVERLORD itself, was Ramsay's operational awareness. In April 1944 he relocated his headquarters to HMS *Dryad*, Southwick House, near Portsmouth so he could be close to the embarkation ports. Southwick House became the nerve centre of SHAEF from late May 1944 when Eisenhower held morning conferences there before heading off to the Allies' Air Headquarters at RAF Uxbridge. Ramsay's operations room had a huge plywood wall map, made and installed by men from Chad Valley, which he used to maintain an operational picture of the movements of the invasion flotilla.

He needed it, for Ramsay faced a monumental task. The entire invasion fleet would be drawn from the Royal Navy (RN), US Navy (USN), Canadian (RCN), Free French, Greek, Dutch and Norwegian navies, and consist of 1,213 warships, 4,126 landing and transport craft, 736 support and 864 merchant ships – in total, just under 7,000 ships manned and supported by 195,700 naval personnel, mainly from the USN and the RN.

Assembling the troops and flotilla in the harbours and ports of the south coast of England was a huge logistical exercise. With security and secrecy paramount in order to obtain surprise, on 1 April 1944 a 10-mile (16-kilometre) deep restricted zone inland from the coast was established from Land's End to The Wash. At D-6 weeks the naval assault and follow-up forces began to assemble in their respective ports, a process that was complete by D-7 days. The troops were sealed into their camps on 26 May. An important factor in the NEPTUNE planning was ensuring that every single vessel was loaded at their embarkation port with the correct tanks, equipment or troops. Then, on D-1 (or for Task Force U in Devon and Cornwall, which had farther to travel to UTAH beach, the evening of D-2), the vessel had to embark at the correct time, then take up the correct tactical order for the landing. Vessels had to maintain their position while entering the swept channels through the minefields and into the stream of craft making their way towards their respective beaches to ensure that the right craft touched down at the right place at the right time.

The actual time the first wave of landing craft hit the beach was designated as H-hour, about 90 minutes after nautical twilight and around four to five hours before high tide, so that the landing would take place on a rising tide. This would allow for 30 minutes of direct attack from the air and direct fire from the warships and equipped landing craft to soften up the enemy defences, maximise the number of vehicles that could

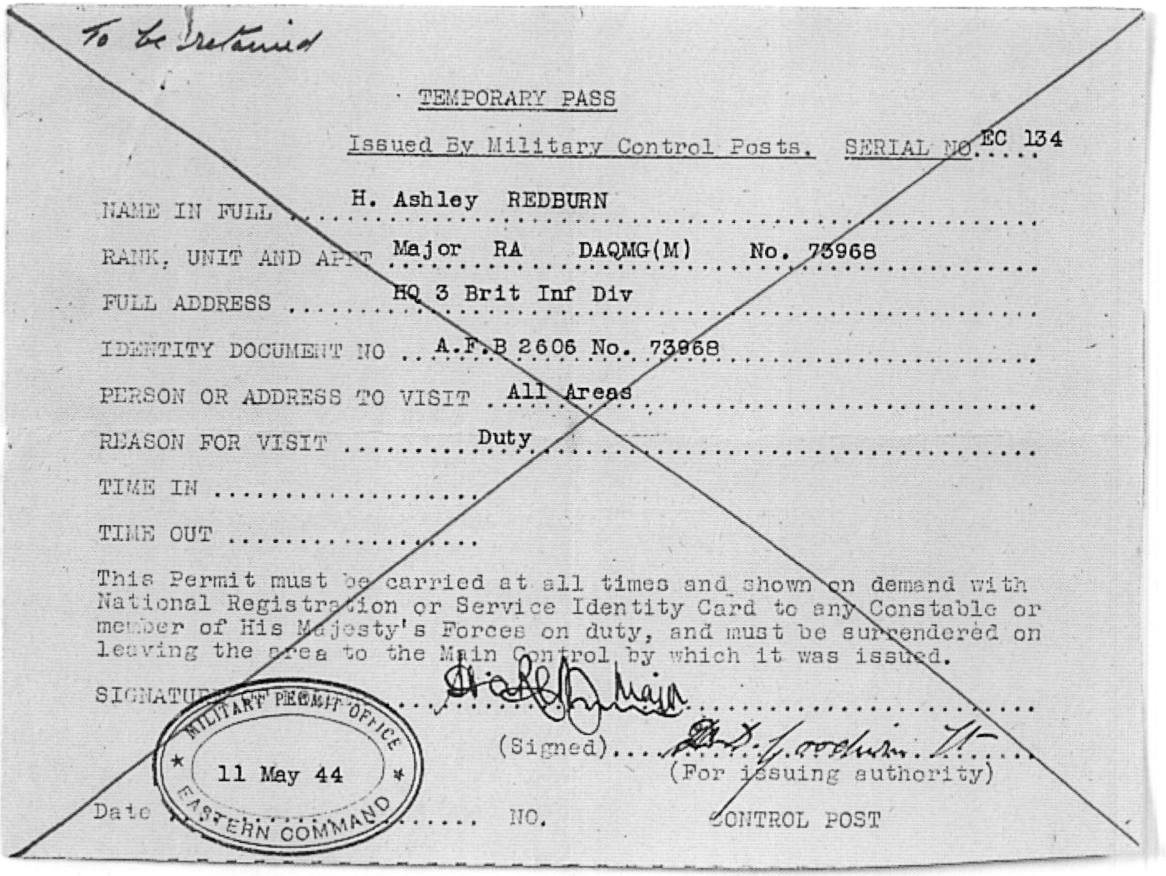

TEMPORARY PASS

Issued By Military Control Posts.   SERIAL NO. EC 134

NAME IN FULL .... H. Ashley REDBURN

RANK, UNIT AND APPT ..... Major RA   DAQMG(M)   No. 73968

FULL ADDRESS .... HQ 3 Brit Inf Div

IDENTITY DOCUMENT NO .... A.F.B 2606 No. 73968

PERSON OR ADDRESS TO VISIT .... All Areas

REASON FOR VISIT .... Duty

TIME IN ....

TIME OUT ....

This Permit must be carried at all times and shown on demand with
National Registration or Service Identity Card to any Constable or
member of His Majesty's Forces on duty, and must be surrendered on
leaving the area to the Main Control by which it was issued.

SIGNATURE ....

(Signed) ....

(For issuing authority)

MILITARY PERMIT OFFICE
★ 11 May 44 ★
EASTERN COMMAND

Date .... NO. .... CONTROL POST

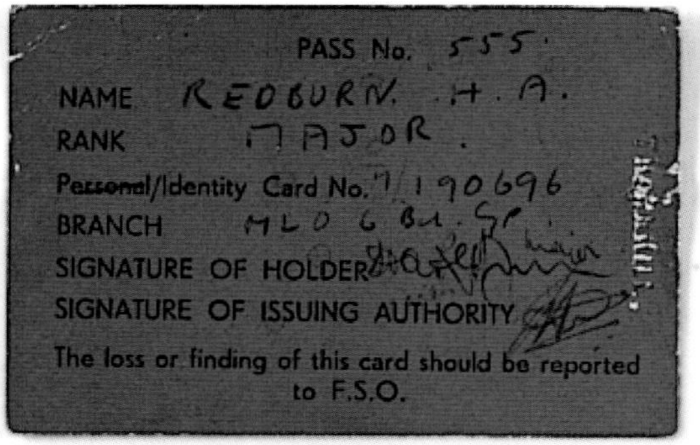

PASS No. 555

NAME   REDBURN. H. A.

RANK   MAJOR.

Personal/Identity Card No. 7190696

BRANCH   MLO 6 Bn. Gp.

SIGNATURE OF HOLDER

SIGNATURE OF ISSUING AUTHORITY

The loss or finding of this card should be reported
to F.S.O.

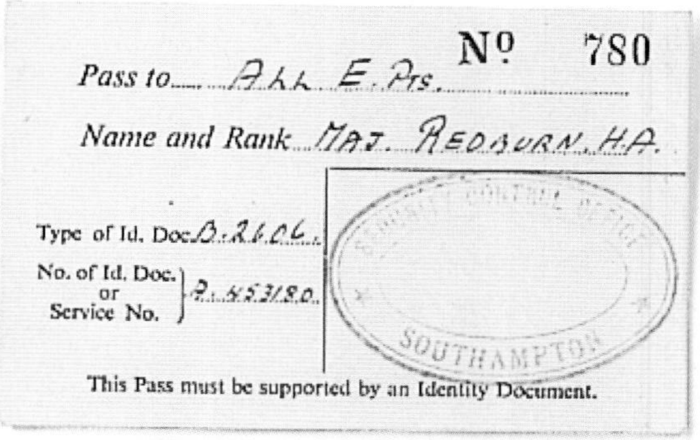

No 780

Pass to ____ All E. Prs.

Name and Rank Maj. Redburn. H.A.

Type of Id. Doc. B.2606

No. of Id. Doc.
    or   } P. 453180.
Service No.

MILITARY CONTROL OFFICE
SOUTHAMPTON

This Pass must be supported by an Identity Document.

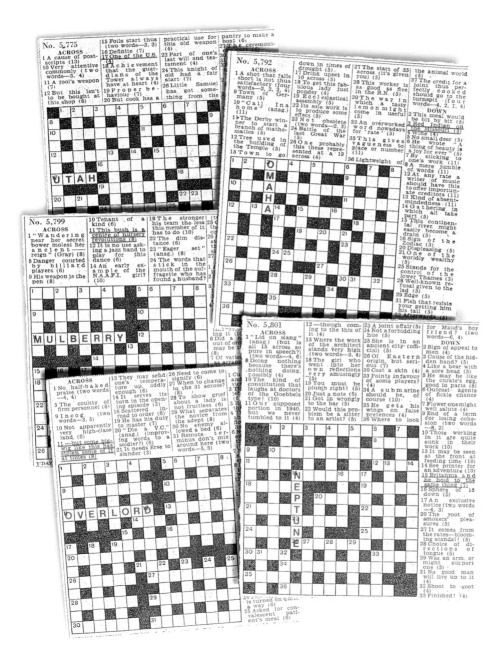

FAR LEFT Security passes issued in May 1944 to Major H.O. Redburn of the Royal Artillery, who was assigned to the quartermaster's department of the British 3rd Division, which was to land on SWORD beach.

LEFT The *Daily Telegraph* crosswords that, between 2 May and 1 June 1944, coincidentally revealed five key codewords in their clues. The innocent puzzle compilers, Sidney Dawe and Melville Jones, were investigated as a result of the bizarre security scare.

ABOVE Insignia of two USAAF units: IX Troop Carrier Command (left) and Glider Airborne Command (right, cap and shoulder insignia respectively).

be landed in the first wave and allow the first wave to land below the first of the beach obstacles. Of course, the plan did not end there. One of the crucial difficulties in amphibious warfare is ownership of the beach, which is after all only a transit area. During D-Day, command of the beach was assigned to naval beachmasters, whose job was to bring order to chaos and maintain the prime objective of getting troops and equipment through and then off the beach zone to start them moving inland.

Once the first wave was ashore and the beaches secure, follow-up forces would land as part of the build-up of troops, equipment and supplies that would be necessary for winning the land battle to link up all the beaches into one coherent front, then to break out of the landing areas and begin the liberation of France. By D+4 the Allies hoped to be landing 58,000 men and 8,000 vehicles each day. The importance of breaking out had been highlighted just a few months before, in February 1944, when the initial Allied landings at Anzio, Italy, had endured four months of attritional combat before breaking out of the beachhead. The OVERLORD plan had pointed to the danger of the Germans stabilising their front around D+14, when SHAEF estimated the Germans could muster 28 divisions against just over 19 Allied divisions. While the Allies could bring more force to bear eventually, that would take time, so key to the campaign was winning the battle to build up forces in Normandy. To achieve that the Allies would continue to attack German communications and reinforcements, as well as launching a secondary invasion in the South of France (Operation DRAGOON) and keeping up the pressure in Italy. But crucial to maintaining Allied momentum in Normandy itself was the fourth phase of the OVERLORD plan.

MULBERRY: This was the continued logistic build-up of Allied forces in France, not just for the invasion but to undertake the liberation of Europe from Nazi occupation. For this, port facilities would be needed. The lesson of the raid on Dieppe in 1942 was that an amphibious assault on a port was hazardous in the extreme and so the Allies' novel idea was to take their own ports to the invasion beaches. The concept of the MULBERRY artificial harbour was born. Two would be built to provide port facilities at OMAHA (Mulberry A) and GOLD (Mulberry B). At a cost of £25 million, MULBERRY was the most ambitious civil engineering project ever undertaken in wartime, clear evidence of the importance placed upon it by Churchill. It took nine months to build and assemble all the component parts. Using over one million tons of steel-reinforced concrete, 147 massive five-storey caissons (PHOENIX) were constructed to be towed across and flooded to provide a harbour wall. Seventy blockships (GOOSEBERRIES) would be sailed to the two sites and scuttled next to the caissons to provide a breakwater. Further out to sea, huge steel crucifixes (BOMBARDONS) were anchored as a first line of defence against the tide and weather. Within the confines of the artificial harbour, an area of around two square miles (five square kilometres) was thereby made safe from the potentially dangerous Channel tides and storms, and artificial roadways (WHALES) would be built on pontoons (BEETLES). Floating pierheads on four legs (SPUDS) would rise and fall on the tide, allowing for continuous unloading of cargo. All this meant that loaded trucks could drive straight off ships, over the beach and into the road network, saving valuable time. In order to maintain a secure supply of fuel, a pipeline (PLUTO) would be laid from the British Isles to the French coast.

The delay

Despite all the planning, training, practice and shaping operations, launching such a massive amphibious assault was still a leap into the unknown and there were some on the Allied side who still had doubts. On 5 June 1944 Field Marshal Lord Alanbrooke, the British Chief of the Imperial General Staff, thought: 'At the best, it will come very far short of the expectations of the bulk of the people, namely all those who know nothing about its difficulties. At its worst, it may well be the most ghastly disaster of the whole war.'

Crucial were accurate weather forecasts which, taking into account tide state, the moon phase and the amount of potential daylight, had identified three days between 5 and 7 June 1944 for the invasion, with Monday 5 June the preferred date. Delayed due to bad weather, some troops already embarked spent an uncomfortable night onboard their vessels. On the evening of 4 June a crucial SHAEF meeting was held in the library at Southwick House. Group Captain James Stagg briefed the assembled commanders on

Harry Bare
Sergeant, Company F, 116th Regimental Combat Team

• •

It was a weird feeling to hear those heavy shells go overhead. Some of the guys were seasick. Others, like myself, just stood there, thinking and shivering. There was a fine rain and a spray, and the boat was beginning to ship water. Still, there was no return fire from the beach, which gave us hope that the navy and the air force had done a good job.

This hope died four hundred yards from the shore.

the likely conditions for Tuesday 6 June. Utilising weather data provided by ships in the Atlantic, Stagg predicted there would be an improvement in the weather that would last 24 hours for 6 June, but conditions would still be marginal. In order for the

troops at sea to remain combat-ready and the airborne armada to begin its journey to the drop and landing zones, the order for the invasion to go ahead had to be given. The only other alternative was to call it off, but as Admiral Ramsay pointed out, if it were delayed again there was no chance of restarting again for 7 June – it would mean a delay of another two weeks. Leigh-Mallory was concerned about visibility and Tedder thought it a risk. Eisenhower asked Montgomery, 'Do you see any reason for not going Tuesday?'; Monty responded with, 'I would say go'. At 21:45 Eisenhower declared, 'I am quite positive that the order must be given'. Eisenhower retired to his trailer for a few hours until a final meeting at 04:00 on 5 June. According to General Bedell Smith, Eisenhower sat in silence for five minutes, knowing the decision was his and his alone. After weighing up all the information and advice, he concluded that the dangers of delay were greater than launching the invasion in the marginal conditions of the 24-hour window predicted by Stagg and said, 'Well, we'll go'. Eisenhower then composed a letter taking personal responsibility if the operation was a failure.

Major Werner Pluskat
352nd Artillery Regiment, 352nd Infantry Division

· ·

As the first grey light of dawn began to creep across the sky I thought I could see something along the horizon. I picked up my artillery binoculars and stepped back with amazement when I saw that the horizon was literally filling with ships of all kinds. I could hardly believe it. It seemed impossible to me that this vast fleet could have gathered without anyone being any wiser.

I passed the binoculars to the man alongside me and said 'Take a look'. He said, 'My God, it's the invasion'. I took one more look, then reached for the telephone and called Major Block, the intelligence officer at the divisional headquarters. 'There must be ten thousand ships out there' I told him. Block said, 'Look Pluskat, are you really sure? The Americans and the British don't have than many ships'. I just said, 'For Christ's sake, come and look for yourself,' and then, because of the disbelief in his voice, I said, 'to hell with you,' and threw down the receiver.

The 'Great Crusade'
Thousands of Allied soldiers, sailors and airmen were beginning what Eisenhower called a 'Great Crusade'. The majority of men were not professional soldiers, but were essentially civilians who had been turned into soldiers for the duration of the war. They had two objectives, to get the job over and done with, and to

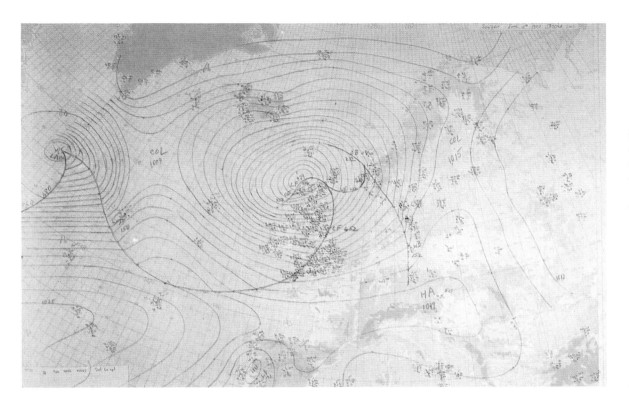

survive. Some were very young, all were either scared or nervous; most were puffing on cigarettes. After crossdecking into their LCAs, some were still ten to 12 miles (16–19 kilometres) from the beaches, so they circled – some for three hours – until the allotted time when they could begin the final run in to the shore. By now many men were being sick into the bags provided, others into their helmets and throwing the contents over the side. For those in the middle of an LCA, that

was not an option; ankle-deep in foul, sloshing, foaming seawater, sick and urine. The men in the assault wave were wet through and overloaded with kit as their LCAs ploughed through the choppy seas. Heavy shells from Allied warships screamed overhead. No fire came from the beaches until the craft were just 400 yards (365 metres) from the shore, recalled Harry Bare of the 116th Regimental Combat Team (RCT), landing at Dog Green sector on OMAHA beach. Then all hell let loose.

PART ONE

THE AMERICAN BEACHES

'There must be ten thousand ships out there...'

Major Werner Pluskat, German 352nd Artillery Regiment.

One of the benefits of the revised COSSAC plan for OVERLORD was the addition of UTAH beach, which would give the Allies a foothold on the Cotentin Peninsula and take them closer to the key port facilities at Cherbourg on D-Day itself. The revised plan called for the US First Army under Lieutenant General Omar Bradley to land Major General J. Lawton Collins's VII Corps at UTAH, while V Corps, under Major General Leonard T. Gerow, landed further east at OMAHA. The landings were scheduled for 06:30.

Cloudy conditions hampered Allied bombers, which failed to destroy many of the German coastal defences, but, with the majority of bombs dropping inland, they did damage some defensive works to the rear, as well as hitting open trenches, barbed wire and some of the German minefields. The Western Task Force under Rear-Admiral Kirk had decided to limit the preparatory bombing and naval gunfire to between nautical twilight and H-40 (H Hour, which was 06:30, minus 40 minutes) to limit the time the Germans would be able to observe the invasion flotilla and the landing of the assault wave.

UTAH and OMAHA were split by the River Vire and hence linking up the American beaches around the town of Carentan would be crucial. A subsidiary factor here was the German gun battery located on Pointe du Hoc, which could fire upon both American beaches. The Germans had flooded the hinterland behind UTAH and routes off the beach would be limited to four causeways. To ensure those were open for the 4th Infantry Division, which was leading the amphibious assault by VII Corps, Mission ALBANY would see the US 101st Airborne Division parachuted in on the night

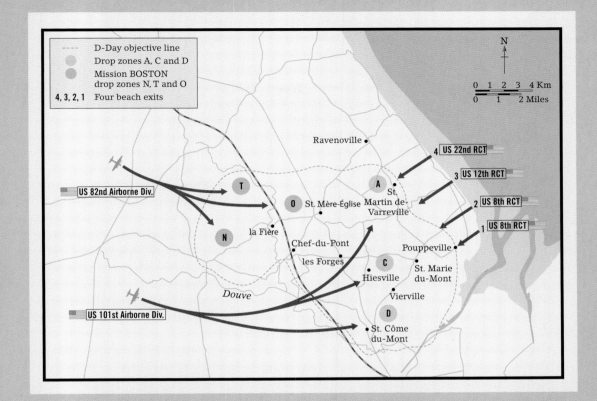

Map Legend

- – – – D-Day objective line
- Drop zones A, C and D
- Mission BOSTON drop zones N, T and O
- 4, 3, 2, 1   Four beach exits

N

0 1 2 3 4 Km
0   1   2 Miles

Ravenoville

US 82nd Airborne Div.

T

O   St. Mère-Église

N

la Fière

Chef-du-Pont

les Forges

Douve

A

St. Martin de-Varreville

4   US 22nd RCT
3   US 12th RCT
2   US 8th RCT
1   US 8th RCT

Pouppeville

C

Hiesville

St. Marie du-Mont

Vierville

D

St. Côme du-Mont

US 101st Airborne Div.

LEFT American operations on the Cherbourg Peninsula, showing the two airborne missions, BOSTON and ALBANY, and the amphibious landing at UTAH beach.

of 5/6 June to land in three drop zones and seize the beach exits, assist with cutting off the peninsula from German reinforcements and help with the reduction of Cherbourg. A little to the west – in Mission BOSTON – the US 82nd Airborne Division would land in three drop zones with the object of taking St. Mère-Église. Both airborne landings would provide depth to the beach landings and reinforcements would arrive later in the day in the form of glider-borne troops.

Landing around 13,000 paratroopers in the same area at around the same time was a considerable logistical undertaking and things did not go according to plan. The C-47 and C-54 transport planes, each carrying a 'stick' of 18–20 paratroopers, took off around midnight. In advance of this main body, special Pathfinder units were parachuted in to use radar beacons and Aldis lamps to guide in the transports. However, cloud cover hampered navigation and many Pathfinders missed

LEFT General Dwight D. Eisenhower talks to American paratroopers at Greenham Common in England on 5 June 1944, just hours before their departure for France. The men are from Company E, 502nd Parachute Infantry Regiment, 101st Airborne Division – the 'Screaming Eagles'. Before Eisenhower, wearing the jumpmaster's tag 23, is Lieutenant Wallace C. ('Wally') Strobel on his 22nd birthday.

their drop zones and had to set up ad-hoc ones where they could. When the air armada hit the cloudbank, the 821 planes lost cohesion. Anti-aircraft fire brought down 21 transports and added to the overall confusion.

Despite the best efforts of many pilots, the airborne formations were dispersed over a wide area as 'sticks' from the 101st started to land around 01:30. In chaotic scenes across the Cotentin, small groups of paratroopers found themselves in hot firefights with German defenders. Some units, such as the 2nd Battalion, 502nd Parachute Infantry Regiment (PIR), landed in the thick Normandy *bocage* and spent most of D-Day trying to gather itself together. In contrast, the landing of the 1/506 and 2/506 PIR saw sufficient concentration of forces to enable the seizure of the two southern beach exits off UTAH. Paratroopers from the 82nd started to land around 02:30 and were, generally, even more dispersed – but with a few crucial exceptions. One of these was the landing of 3/505 PIR to the northwest of St. Mère-Église, allowing the unit commander Lieutenant Colonel Krause to gather 180 paratroopers and assault and seize the town.

The American airborne landings were so dispersed and seeming to lack coordination that the unintended consequence was the Germans could not fathom if they were a diversion or the first part of an Allied assault on Normandy. As a consequence their response lacked speed and coordination, which allowed the paratroopers to secure (by 13:00) the four UTAH beach exits and to establish a defensive perimeter for the beach landings of the 4th Infantry Division. When the counter-attacks came – for instance at St. Mère-Église around 09:30, or later in the day on the River Merderet around 14:00 – the Americans held on. This provided a foothold for both the glider supports, arriving during the day, as well as the 4th Division and the rest of the VII Corps coming over UTAH beach.

The American airborne divisions did achieve their wider objects on D-Day, but at a terrible cost. By the end of 6 June the 101st could only muster just over a third of its original strength of 6,600 men, having suffered 182 killed, 557 wounded and 501 missing.

Carl Cartledge
501st Parachute Infantry Regiment:

• •

[Flying out of Welford Airfield, Cartledge was one of a 'stick' of 23 American paratroopers on a C-47 (USAAF Skytrain, RAF Dakota), as they crossed the French countryside:]

Immediately, I was hit by the strong odor of gunsmoke, and ahead of us was a sea of tracers thick enough to walk on. There was no way we were not going to be hit.

No one had to tell us what it was when we heard it for the first time. It sounded like rocks in a tin can when the bullets hit the aircraft. Our plane began to take evasive action…. three of our forty-five planes were shot down.

The green light popped on – 'Go, Geronimo!' And we all jumped. I've never been so glad to get out of an airplane in my whole life. The parachute slammed open; the planes were gone, taking the tracers with them.

There was water everywhere below, expect just a small strip that I could see, and I was drifting dangerously close to the water. I pushed my thumbs into the saddle of the chute and sat down and quickly unbuckled my leg straps, preparing for a water landing. I was working on my chest straps when my shoe caught a small tree and I smashed into marshy ground….There was no sound from the water. It was obvious to us that the first twelve men of plane 44 had drowned.

ABOVE AND RIGHT The helmet, jump jacket, belt and equipment worn by General James M. Gavin, 502nd Parachute Infantry Regiment and assistant commander of the US 82nd Airborne Division on D-Day. Gavin, a pioneer of airborne warfare who was nicknamed 'Jumpin' Jim', was promoted to command the 82nd in August 1944. In Sicily in 1943 he had earned the first of two Distinguished Service Crosses and become the US Army's youngest major general. He made more combat jumps (four) than any American general of the war. On D-Day his message to the Pathfinders he had helped to establish was sombre: 'When you land in Normandy you will have only one friend: God.'

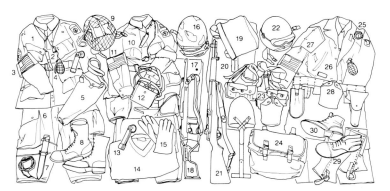

AMERICAN AIRBORNE UNIFORMS AND ACCOUTREMENTS

1. M1942 paratroop jump jacket with the insignia of 82nd Airborne Division
2. M2 pocket knife and the ACME No. 470 clicker, a nighttime signaller developed for D-Day and known as the 'cricket' by the men of the airborne brotherhood
3. Oilcloth arm brassard
4. Mk. 2 grenade
5. Training gas mask in a case
6. M1942 jump pants
7. M3 knife with M8 scabbard
8. Leather jump boots
9. M1C helmet with chin cup and first aid packet
10. M1942 officer's jump jacket
11. Formation ID brassard
12. Binoculars (6×30) with case
13. Hand torch TL-122-C
14. OD (olive drab) wool sweater
15. Leather airborne gloves
16. M1C helmet camouflaged
17. Carbine jump bag
18. M1A1 .30in calibre carbine with folding wire stock
19. Assault gas mask and case
20. Griswold padded bag to contain a disassembled M1 rifle
21. M1 .30in calibre Garand rifle
22. M1C helmet with the insignia of 328th Glider Infantry Regiment and M1944 goggles for glider troops
23. M1926 cartridge belt with M1936 combat suspenders, M1919 entrenching tool with cover and improved M1910 canteen and cover
24. M1936 canvas bag with poncho
25. Wrist compass
26. M1941 OD field jacket with wool field trousers
27. Gas brassard
28. M1936 pistol belt carrying a leather holster, containing the M1911A1 pistol, and M1938 wire cutters and case
29. M1938 canvas leggings
30. Service boots

UTAH BEACH

Spearheading the US Army's VII Corps' assault on UTAH beach were four companies of the 8th Regimental Combat Team (RCT), 4th Infantry Division. An American RCT had its supporting arms embedded into the formation and was the equivalent strength of three British infantry battalions. The regiment would land line abreast at two sectors, Uncle Red and Tare Green, providing swift access to beach exits 3 and 4. The RCTs were supported by DD tanks of the 70th Tank Battalion. Apart from the airborne landings already underway in missions BOSTON and ALBANY, other elements of VII Corps had already been in action, with men from the 4th and 24th Cavalry Squadrons seizing the islands of St. Marcouf.

At 05:30 Task Force U came under fire from German coastal batteries and, while manoeuvring, the destroyer USS *Corry* hit a mine. The rest of the large warships, including HMS *Black Prince* and the huge American battleship USS *Nevada*, opened up a preparatory

'We're going to start the war from right here.'

Brigadier General Theodore Roosevelt Jr, Assistant
Division Commander, 4th Infantry Division

UTAH BEACH FACT FILE

OBJECT	To establish a bridgehead along the line Quineville–St. Mère-Église, north of Carentan; link up with (US) 82nd and 101st Airborne; establish bridgeheads over the canal and River Vire in preparation for linking up with US V Corps at OMAHA.
NAVAL FORCE	'U', Rear-Admiral D.P. Moon on USS *Bayfield*.
ASSAULT FORCE	(US) 4th Infantry Division (VII Corps), Major General Raymond Barton.
LANDING TIME	06:30

• •

01:15–01:30	Airborne landings by US 82nd and 101st Airborne Divisions commence to provide depth to UTAH and secure the causeway exits from the beach.
04:30	The Isles St. Marcouf are occupied by 4th and 24th Cavalry Squadrons.
05:40	*PC 1261* hits a mine, landing craft start to veer off course.
05:50	Naval bombardment begins.
06:05–06:24	525 tons of bombs dropped by Allied bombers.
06:30	8th Regimental Combat Team (RCT) hits the beach 2,000 yards (1,830 metres) south of the intended landing zone.
06:40	28 DD tanks arrive on the beach, German opposition is light.
08:00	Brigadier General Theodore Roosevelt Jr orders follow-on formations to land at the new landing zone.
09:00	Beach 2 becomes the main route off UTAH.
10:00	Six battalions landed, including follow-up troops from the 12th and 22nd Regimental Combat Teams.
12:00	Troops from UTAH start linking up with the airborne forces inland, providing depth to the initial assault.
24:00	Perimeter 4 miles (6 kilometres) inland of UTAH established; 23,250 troops are ashore for only 197 casualties. US airborne losses are considerably greater – 2,499 casualties, including 338 killed.

'We're going to start the war from right here'. Roosevelt was later awarded the Congressional Medal of Honor for his leadership at UTAH beach.

Once *WN*5 had been neutralised men could start to move inland using beach exit 2, which was secure by 09:00. Now the main threat was from German minefields as men snaked in single file through the sand dunes following narrow paths cleared by the combat engineers. 'Watch yourself, fella. That's a mine', a soldier lying on the ground warned Treanor, who recalled: 'He had one foot half blown off…while he waited for the litter-bearers, he was warning other soldiers about the mines in that vicinity.'

At H+85 minutes the 22nd Infantry Regiment was landed, followed at H+4 hours by the 12th Infantry Regiment. Both were directed to the northern part of UTAH to assist with their object of linking up with the 101st Airborne. Meanwhile, the 3rd Battalion 8th RCT had pushed west, fought and won a brisk engagement with elements of the 919th Grenadier Regiment before linking up with the 82nd Airborne. By the close of 6 June the VII Corps had been unable to extend its bridgehead over the River Merderet; pockets of enemy resistance continued to the south and east of St. Mère-Église and US forces were still several miles from Carentan. Yet, the UTAH landing had been a great

ABOVE US insignia, clockwise, from top left: 82nd Airborne Division, XVII Airborne Corps, 101st Airborne Division, and the Engineer, Navy and Army amphibious units.

LEFT Soldiers with the United States Navy (USN) 2nd Beach Battalion inspect radio-operated German beetle, or Goliath, 'tracked mines' captured on UTAH during D-Day.

success. By the end of the day the entire 4th Division was ashore, along with the initial elements of the follow-up 90th Division: over 23,000 men, 1,700 vehicles and 1,700 tons of stores. VII Corps had reached its D-Day objectives and, considering the problems faced (some of which turned out to be of positive benefit), had established a beachhead, with some room for manoeuvre and the continued build-up required to push into the Cotentin Peninsula for the loss of just 197 men.

RIGHT United States Navy (USN) uniforms and equipment. Clockwise, from top left: M1 steel helmet in USN grey with added combat art; dungaree work uniform with M1943 service shoes, and the earphones, microphone and steel talker's helmet used by a guncrew chief (with detail, opposite); M1938 leggings and ID tags of a member of the 28th USN Construction Battalion – the famous CBs or 'Seabees' – at Cherbourg; and an M1 helmet, M1936 pistol belt with an M1910 canteen and a cover, with a USN M1 knife and sheath.

RIGHT Some German items picked up by Allied soldiers on the assault beaches. Beneath the two family letters and a gravity knife is a rifle bayonet, retrieved during the push through one of the landing beaches. The soldier's ring (top) was found at Port-en-Bessin. At top right are two books: (top) a *wehrpass* issued to Georg Lahs, a gunner from Bonn, and (bottom) a *soldbuch* issued to Kanonier Wilhelm Gloystein, a gunner from Oldenburg, which records details of leave, travel and issue of kit.

LEFT AND ABOVE All these items belonged to Lieutenant Joseph McFalls, commanding officer of *LCT 474*, which operated off UTAH and OMAHA beaches. In early May 1944 McFalls had picked up, in this delivery bag, the NEPTUNE orders from Plymouth when he acted as courier for LCT groups 10, 11 and 12. During the landings, McFalls was holding the code book (top right) in his hand when a near miss shredded the book and blew him off the bridge into the LCT, causing wounds for which he was awarded the Purple Heart (top left and detail, opposite).

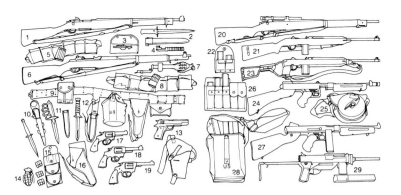

AMERICAN ARMS AND EQUIPMENT

1 M1903A3 Springfield .30in calibre (.30-06, or M1906 cartridge) rifle

2 Bayonet and scabbard for the M1930A3 and M1 rifles

3 M15 grenade launcher sight and case

4 M1903A1 rifle's grenade launcher

5 M1903A3 rifle's 12-clip bandolier

6 M1 Garand .30in (M1906 cartridge) calibre semi-automatic rifle

7 Mk. IIA1 grenade with projector adapter M1A2 and launcher M7

8 M1 Garand six-clip bandolier

9 M1936 pistol belt with the M1942 first aid pouch, M1916 hip holster, M1910 canteen (modified) and M1918 web magazine pocket

10 Fairbairn-Sykes knife

11 M1918 Mk. 1 fighting knife

12 M3 fighting knife and M8 sheath

13 M1911A1 pistol and M3 shoulder holster

14 Mk. IIA1 grenade

15 Pouch for 18 rounds of M1917 revolver ammunition

16 M1917 holster

17 Smith and Wesson Victory Model revolver

18 Smith and Wesson M1917 Army revolver

19 Colt M1917 Army revolver

20 M1903A4 sniper .30in rifle with Weaver M73B1 sight

21 M1 .30in calibre carbine

22 Carbine clip pouch

23 M1A1 carbine with folding wire 'airborne' stock

24 M1928A1 Thompson submachine gun

25 M1928A1's 50-round drum

26 Pouch for five 20-round clips for the Thompson M1

27 Thompson M1 submachine gun

28 Ammunition bag

29 M3 submachine gun

LEFT A selection of shoulder and breast patches belonging to American war correspondents and photographers. Although they were non-combatants, accredited correspondents wore uniforms – such as a khaki or olive drab jacket (opposite), with a helmet or beret – and risked life and limb to report from the war zone. After 6 June, as details of the invasion and the forces involved began to be published, all photographs of the invasion beaches had to be passed by a military censor.

OMAHA BEACH

L anding at OMAHA was an operational necessity to provide a broad front to the invasion by linking with the Anglo-Canadian beaches SWORD, GOLD and JUNO. It would also minimise the risk that UTAH would be cut off from the rest of the landings. OMAHA was selected as the location for the construction of MULBERRY A. OMAHA required a supporting operation to assault the German battery on the Pointe du Hoc, three and a half miles (5.5 kilometres) to the west. There, 200 Germans of the 716th Static Infantry Regiment had been casemating six 155mm guns, which could fire upon both UTAH and OMAHA beaches. Following an air and naval bombardment, three companies of 2nd US Rangers climbed waterlogged ropes and assaulted the 100-foot (30-metre) cliffs around 07:10 under covering from HMS *Talybont* and USS *Saterlee*. They found the gun positions empty. Taking the initiative, the US Rangers eventually found four of the 155mm guns inland and destroyed them, before creating a defensive perimeter on the Pointe. By D+1, of the 225 Rangers in the assault force, over 60 per cent had become casualties.

Comprising a gently curving shingle beach overlooked by bluffs, with only five draws or exits off the beach for vehicles, OMAHA was the most

OMAHA BEACH FACT FILE

OBJECT	To establish control of RN 13 between Isigny and Bayeux. Two US Ranger battalions were allotted for the capture of Pointe du Hoc.
NAVAL FORCE	'O' Rear-Admiral J.L. Hall on USS *Ancon*.
ASSAULT FORCE	(US) 1st Infantry Division (V Corps), Major General C.R. Heubner (116th RCT, 29th Division, attached).
LANDING TIME	06:30

• •

05:35	DD tanks are launched too far out, 27 sink.
05:45–06:25	Naval bombardment fails to hit defensive bunkers.
06:00	Bombers drop their payloads inland.
06:31	First assault wave lands, but in some cases suffers very heavy losses, especially at Dog Green.
07:00	With heavy losses to junior officers and NCOs, chaos reigns and the assault is pinned on the beach.
07:10	2nd US Rangers assaults Pointe du Hoc. Having scaled 100-foot (30-metre) cliffs, they find the gun positions empty. The guns are found inland and destroyed; pockets of resistance until D+1.
07:30	Second assault wave starts to land at OMAHA, creating a crowded and confused situation. Brigadier General Norman D. Cota lands.
07:40	5th US Rangers land near Les Moulins draw.
08:00	The rising tide starts to drown many wounded men.
08:30	Beachmaster judges it vital to stop further landings.
09:00	*WN*60 is captured, the first German position to fall.
09:30	Germans assess the OMAHA landing to have failed.
10:00	Cota organises attacks on Vierville-sur-Mer, leading to its capture around 11:00.
12:25	Although defences at OMAHA are penetrated, German reinforcements are sent to GOLD beach.
14:00	Engineers blow the anti-tank wall at the Vierville-sur-Mer draw. By 17:00 the draw is open to vehicles.
24:00	Thin beachhead established, only 1.5 miles (1 kilometre) deep, at the cost of 2,400 casualties – yet 34,250 men had been landed by the end of 6 June.

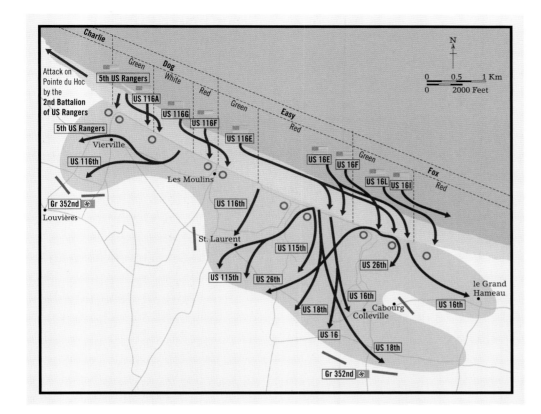

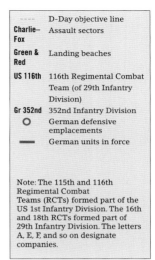

LEFT OMAHA beach and the landing of the 1st US Infantry Division and the 29th Division of V Corps. Note the limited penetration inland (denoted by the highlighted area) on D-Day itself.

formidable position on the Normandy coastline. Taking advantage of the natural terrain, it was heavily protected by German defences that included 12 strongpoints and 60 artillery pieces, as well as numerous mortars and machine guns. Initially manned by two battalions of the 726th Infantry Regiment from the 716th Infantry Division, in March the defences had been reinforced by the 914th and 916th Grenadier Regiments from the 352nd Division, with other parts

of the division held in reserve. In fact, in the early hours of 6 June the reserve units had been sent off to the west to respond to the American airborne landings and were therefore, fortunately for the Americans, unable to reinforce the beach defences. In *Widerstandsnest* (*WN*) 62, defending what the Americans designated as the Easy Red sector, was Franz Gockel. This strongpoint, on the edge of the Coleville-sur-Mer draw (the main exit off the beach through the cliff), housed two 75mm

LEFT Landing craft and a fleet of protection vessels approach OMAHA beach on 6 June 1944, revealing the immense scale of the Allied undertaking. Omaha Beach saw the toughest fighting and the most Allied losses of the four beaches assaulted that day.

guns sited for enfilade fire along the beach. They, in turn, were protected by an anti-tank ditch and a minefield, and supported by two 50mm guns in open stands, a 50mm mortar and at least five MG42 machine guns. Trenches and Tobruks (concrete foxholes, which might house a tank turret, machine-gun nest or mortar pit) sited in the bluffs were manned by infantry and, after emerging unscathed following the air and naval bombardment, Gockel waited patiently for the landing troops to enter his pre-set defensive fire zones.

The initial assault – by the 16th RCT from the 1st Infantry Division in the eastern sectors and the 116th

RCT from the 29th Division in the western sectors – would hit the beach at 06:30 accompanied by the 5th and 6th Provisional Special Engineer Brigades, in total composing around a third of the assault troops. They would use explosives and bulldozers to clear obstacles and, if all went to plan, have the exits open by 08:30.

Due to cloud cover, the majority of bombs dropped by 480 B-17 bombers fell inland. Naval gunfire provided some support while landing craft made their way to the beach, but the 9,000 3-inch rockets fired fell short into the sea. The heavy sea state and the fear of mines caused DD tanks to be launched too far out to sea: in the western sector, 27 of the 32 DD tanks sank on launch. In the eastern sector, however, all the DD tanks were landed by their Landing Craft Tanks (LCTs) at the local commander's initiative, but arrived *after* the infantry.

Twenty landing craft out of the assault wave of 200 were lost before the force reached the beach. In the heavy swell, smoke and spray made navigation difficult and infantry companies arrived out of place; Frank Simeone, of Company G, 116th RCT, landed 1,000 yards (915 metres) to the east of the Vierville-sur-Mer draw. As ramps dropped on LCAs the worst hit were those landing at Dog Green, where Company A of the 116th RCT was virtually wiped out, sustaining 96 per cent casualties, and Companies A and B of the 2nd US Rangers also suffered many. Three LCTs were hit by shells from the two German 88mm guns located in *WN*72 by the Vierville-sur-Mer draw. The combat engineers in the first wave, who were supposed to be

'There are two kinds of people who are staying on this beach: those who are dead and those who are going to die. Now let's get the hell out of here.'

Colonel George Taylor, 16th RCT, OMAHA beach.

clearing beach obstacles, sustained over 40 per cent casualties and only three of the 16 combat bulldozers made it to the beach. Here, unlike the British, the American decision not to use flail tanks and other specialist armoured engineer tanks was detrimental as clearing German wire, minefields and pillboxes by hand was not only costly but very time-consuming.

Many American junior officers and NCOs were casualties and in the confusion paralysis gripped many on the beach as men bunched up, unable to provide mutual support. They proved to be perfect targets for the German MG42 machine guns sited to maximise crossfires. Harry Parley of Company E, 116th RCT, thought the machine-gun fire made a 'sip-sip sound, like someone sucking on their teeth'. Luck was a significant factor for many who survived. Compared to the fate of the 116th, a group from the 2nd Battalion 16th RCT had landed between Coleville-sur-Mer and St. Laurent, crossing the beach and suffering only two casualties. Here the naval gunfire support and grassfire smoke helped open a path for Lieutenant Spaulding

Robert Slaughter

Age 19, Heavy Weapons Sergeant, Company D,
1st Battalion, 116th RCT, 29th Division

• •

As we approached the beach the ramp was lowered. Mortar and artillery shells exploded on land and in the water. Unseen snipers concealed in the cliffs were shooting down at individuals, but most of the havoc was from automatic weapons. The water was turning red from blood. Explosions from artillery gunfire, the rapid-fire rattle from nearby MG-42s, and naval gunfire firing inland was frightening.

There were dead men floating in the water and there were live men acting dead, letting the tide take them in...

While lying half in and half out of the water behind one of the log poles, I noticed a GI running from right to left trying to get across the beach. He was weighted with equipment and looked as though he was having a difficult time running....An enemy gunner shot him as he stumbled for cover. He screamed for a medic. One of the aid men moved quickly to help him and he was also shot. I will never forget seeing that medic lying next to that wounded GI and both of them screaming. They died in minutes.

I ran as low as I could to lessen the target, and since I am 6ft 5in I still presented a good one....We were loaded down with gear and soaking wet. ...As I ran through a tidal pool with about 6 or 8 inches of water, I began to stumble. I finally caught my balance and accidentally fired my rifle, barely missing my foot.

to lead 16 men to the top of the bluffs as early as 07:50, where they started to clear the enemy trench system, which was largely manned by Polish conscripts.

The second wave of assault forces started to arrive at 07:30 and it sustained heavy losses. Wrecked ships and vehicles and mangled corpses began to pile up in the rising surf. Responding to this inertia, Brigadier General Norman D. Cota of the 29th Division, who had waded ashore, took tactical charge of a group of men of the 116th, supported by men of the 2nd Rangers, at the Vierville-sur-Mer draw. Cota directed covering fire and the laying of Bangalore torpedoes to blow gaps in the barbed wire. The first man through was hit and Cota took it upon himself to lead the troops up the bluffs before heading back to the beach.

After 08:00 USN destroyers, on the initiative of their commanders, began to close towards the shore to provide direct fire support, but with chaos reigning on the beach at 08:30 the naval beachmaster on OMAHA suspended further landings as General Bradley began to consider sending the follow-on waves to the other beaches. With the sea foam stained red 'bloody OMAHA' was quickly turning into a butcher's shambles. At 09:30 the German commander at the Pointe et Raz de la Percée judged the landing to have failed.

With chaos on the beach and at sea, where the landing order had become muddled, at Vierville-sur-Mer Cota climbed the bluffs once more and found the men he had assembled pinned down. 'Ok, now let's see what you're made of', he yelled, and led a charge, pistol in hand, to penetrate the German positions, finally stumbling onto a road parallel to the beaches. Cota followed this and it led to the heights above the draw, which finally enabled the Americans to force out some of the German defenders. A number of disparate groups now started to assemble around Cota, including Colonel Charles Canham of the 116th RCT, who had also worked his way up the bluffs. 'Where the hell have you been, boys?' Cota inquired of Company C, 116th RCT, as he stood twirling his .45 Colt automatic.

Cota, reassuming his command responsibilities, managed to regain radio contact with the fleet and indicate that some progress was being made, before organising an engineer assault on Vierville-sur-Mer draw's anti-tank barrier, which was only partially successful because the remaining equipment could not penetrate the concrete. USN destroyers closed to 550 yards (500 metres) of the shore and poured in fire, often taking their targets from armour and infantry fire: 3,500 shells were fired between 10:00 and 11:00. By 11:00 the Vierville-sur-Mer *WN*s had been destroyed by a combination of naval gunfire and infantry assault, but the draw itself was not opened for vehicles until 17:00, over eight and a half hours behind schedule.

More than 35,000 men had been landed at OMAHA by the end of D-Day, although the deepest penetration inland was only 1 mile (1.6 kilometres). US casualties were over 2,400 and the beach was not finally clear of obstacles and enemy artillery fire until 8 June. The German 352nd Division lost about 1,200 of its

3,000 men on D-Day; the reserve units, delayed by the reports of paratrooper landings to the west, arrived piecemeal. Major reserves had been directed towards GOLD beach, which the Germans saw as more important, both in terms of the scale of assault and location.

BELOW A beach invasion sign. In the USA many newspaper editors were even stricter than the government censors. John Steinbeck explained the role of self-censorship among reporters: 'We felt responsible to what was called the home front. There was a general feeling that unless the home front was carefully protected from the whole account of what war was like, it might panic. Also, we felt we had to protect the armed services from criticism, or they might retire to their tents to sulk like Achilles.'

ABOVE Invasion currency signed by officers of the 5th US Ranger Battalion on HMS *Leopold* prior to the landings on OMAHA: Lieutenant Pepper, Lieutenant Shaddock, Captain Whittington, Captain Heffelfinger, Lieutenant Anderson (killed on D-Day), Captain Byren, Lieutenant Zepelski and Lieutenant Colonel Schneider.

LEFT Scaling equipment of the US Rangers. These four- and six-prong grapnel hooks were used by the 2nd US Ranger Battalion in their audacious assault on Pointe du Hoc. The objects were recovered from the area after the battle.

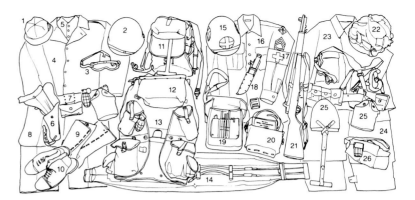

AMERICAN ASSAULT TROOPS' UNIFORMS AND ACCOUTREMENTS

1 M1941 cap for the M1 helmet

2 M1 helmet with the insignia of the 29th Infantry Division

3 M1944 goggles

4 M1941 field jacket

5 M1943 high neck sweater

6 M1911A1 .45in calibre pistol in waterproof cover

7 M1936 pistol belt with leather holster, M1910 canteen, Mk. II fragmentation grenade and M1942 first aid pouch

8 Olive Drab (OD) wool trousers

9 M1938 canvas leggings

10 Service shoes

11 M1928 field pack with M1910 entrenching tool

12 Assault gas mask and case

13 Assault vest, developed for the Normandy landings

14 M26 inflatable life preserver issued to invasion troops

15 M1 helmet with medical ID

16 OD wool shirt with 4th Infantry Division shoulder patch

17 Red Cross brassard

18 Privately purchased fighting knife and sheath

19 M1938 dispatch case

20 First aid pouch

21 M1 Garand .30in calibre carbine

22 M1 helmet with netting and burlap (sacking) camouflage

23 M1943 camouflage jacket of herringbone twill – an item quickly withdrawn from Normandy service because it was too similar to Waffen-SS camouflage uniforms

24 Trousers for the M1943 jacket

25 M1936 suspenders, M1923 cartridge belt, modified M1910 canteen with cover and M1910 entrenching tool with cover

26 Ammunition bandolier (to hold six clips) with an eight-round clip of .30in M1 rifle ammunition

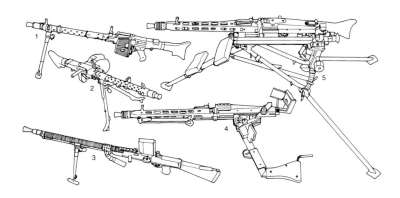

GERMAN MACHINE GUNS

1 Model 1934/41
  Maschinengewehr 34/41
  (MG34) 7.92mm calibre
  with bipod in forward
  (assault) position and basket
  drum (Gurttrommel 34)
  containing a 50-round
  belt of ammunition

2 MG34 with bipod in rear
  (defensive) position and
  50-round drum attached

3 Czech Maschinengewehr
  ZB26(t) 7.92mm calibre
  with 20-round detachable
  magazine – the weapon
  on which the British Bren
  gun was based (the Czech
  manufacturer's name can
  be seen on the side 'BRNO')

4 MG42 7.92mm calibre, a later
  and heavier version of the
  MG34, with special periscope
  optics, stock and trigger group
  that allowed the gunner to
  operate the weapon from a
  concealed position such as
  a trench – the MG42's high
  rate of fire (1,200 rounds per
  minute) was about double that
  of a comparable Allied machine
  gun, which made it a potentially
  devastating weapon to be pitted
  against

5 MG42 7.92mm calibre with
  high-quality Zielfernrohr
  40 optical sight, as used in
  the heavy machine gun role,
  mounted on a tripod (Lafette 42)

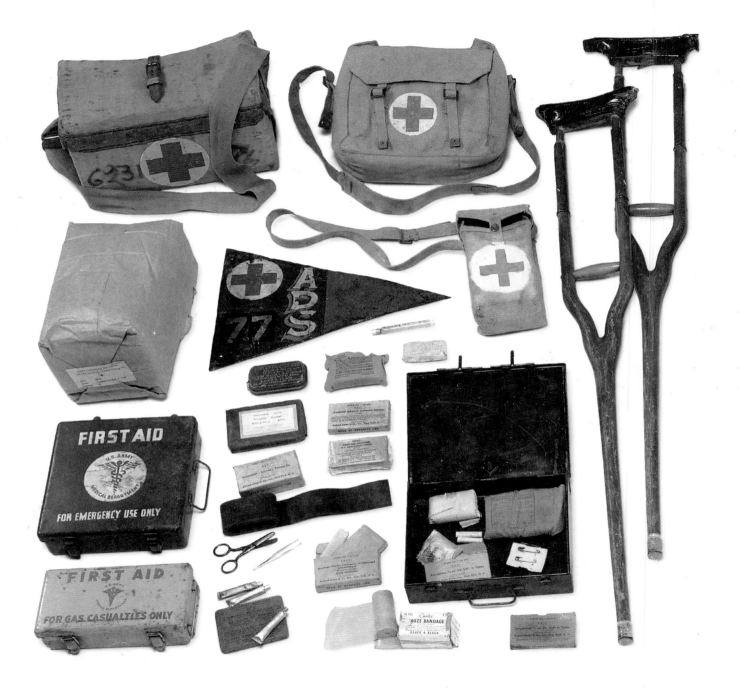

LEFT A poignant reminder of the terrible events on OMAHA, this US Army chaplain's stole and service Bible was found on the beach on 7 June by Stoker James Cook, a crewman of Royal Navy *LST 367*. Four chaplains served with the US 1st Infantry Division on the beach that day, ministering to the wounded and dying. One chaplain on OMAHA, Father Joe Lacy, was even awarded the Distinguished Service Cross for his 'heroic and dauntless actions'.

LEFT This selection of Allied medical supplies and equipment ranges from crutches, from a British hospital in Bayeaux, to scissors and forceps. At the top are first aid bags and satchels. The triangular object is a metal unit location sign for the Canadian 77th Advanced Dressing Station.

Next to it is a plain package containing American Red Cross bandages. Directly beneath the sign are bandages, dressings, a tourniquet, ammonia inhalant, anti-gas ointment and petroleum ointment. On either side are American and British first aid kits.

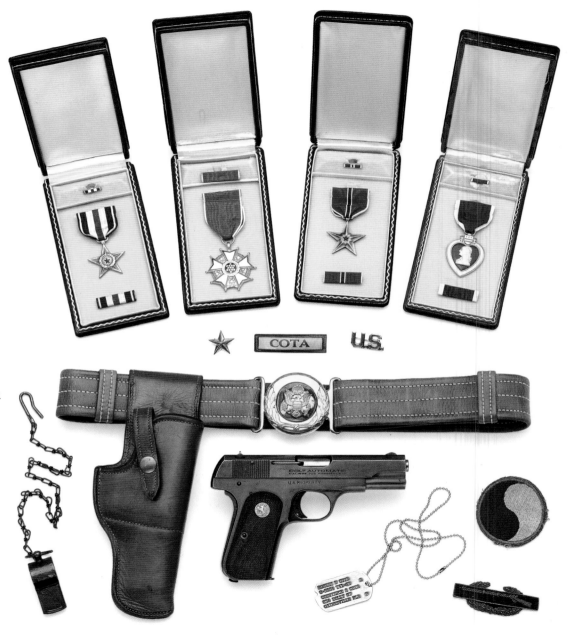

RIGHT Memorabilia of General Norman S. Cota, who was the Assistant Division Commander of the 29th Infantry Division. He went ashore at OMAHA at 07:30 with the 116th Infantry Regiment. At the top, from left to right, are his decorations: Silver Star, Legion of Merit, Bronze Star and Purple Heart with service ribbons and lapel rosettes in their original presentation cases. Beneath those are his collar insignia: silver star, name tag and 'US' device. At the bottom (with detail, opposite), from the left are: his brass command whistle, Colt M380 pocket automatic with general's waist belt and holster, 'dog tags', division shoulder patch and his silver bullion Combat Infantryman's badge.

PART TWO

THE BRITISH AND CANADIAN BEACHES

'... the most impressive piece of flying in the war'

Air Chief Marshal Sir Trafford Leigh-Mallory

W hile the American First Army was landing to the west, the British Second Army would land at three beaches along 20 miles (32 kilometres) of coastline from Port-en-Bessin in the west to the River Orne and Canal in the east. The British XXX Corps' 50th Northumbrian Division would – after landing at GOLD, the westernmost beach, forcing their way ashore and heading inland – take the town of Bayeux, before linking up with I Corps, which was landing at JUNO and SWORD beaches. The Canadian 3rd Division landing at JUNO would head for the airfield at Carpiquet, while the British 3rd Division landing at SWORD would link up with the British 6th Airborne Division, dropped between the rivers Orne and Dives. The Canadians and British would take the city of Caen on D-Day itself to prevent the Germans using it as a hinge to their

expected counter-attack. Having achieved all this, the British Second Army would then be in a suitable position to commence operations towards Paris.

Unlike the American beaches, where the air and naval bombardments were limited to 40 minutes, the Eastern Task Force under Rear-Admiral Vian was scheduled to provide two hours of softening-up fire, while the tide dictated landing times of 07:25 at GOLD and SWORD with a further 10–20-minute delay at JUNO due to a rocky outcrop offshore. There were further differences between the American and British/Canadian approaches, most notably the use of Major General Sir Percy Hobart's range of 'funnies', such as flail tanks, Armoured Vehicle Royal Engineers (AVRE) and 'Crocodile' flame-throwing tanks. Although Bradley did take some DD tanks, American doctrine stressed

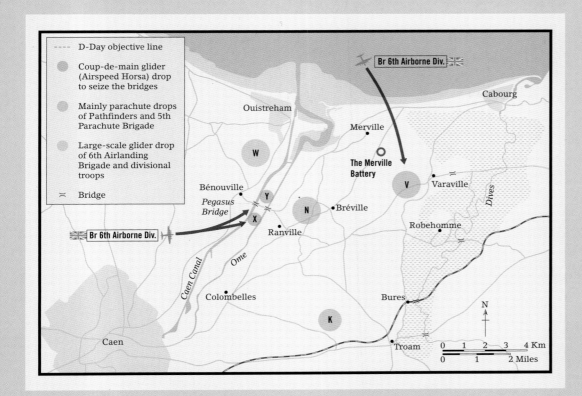

Legend:
- - - - D-Day objective line
- Coup-de-main glider (Airspeed Horsa) drop to seize the bridges
- Mainly parachute drops of Pathfinders and 5th Parachute Brigade
- Large-scale glider drop of 6th Airlanding Brigade and divisional troops
⋈ Bridge

Br 6th Airborne Div.

Cabourg

Ouistreham

Merville

The Merville Battery

Varaville

Dives

Bénouville

Pegasus Bridge

Y

N

Bréville

V

Robehomme

X

Ranville

W

Br 6th Airborne Div.

Caen Canal

Orne

Colombelles

Bures

Caen

K

Troam

N

0 1 2 3 4 Km
0   1   2 Miles

LEFT The British airborne landings, showing the coup-de-main at Pegasus Bridge and the attack on the Merville Battery.

the use of combat engineers rather than armoured vehicles, the consequences of which were evident at OMAHA. Commando units would operate on the flanks of the main British and Canadian landing forces to start to link up the three beaches.

Adding SWORD to the OVERLORD plan brought the landings within easy reach of the 21st Panzer Division. The British 6th Airborne Division, which included the 1st Canadian Parachute Battalion, was to secure the eastern flank of the Allied assault by adding operational depth to cover the naval landings. It would achieve this by seizing vital crossing points in the marshy terrain. This would delay any counter-strike by the armour of the 21st Panzer Division, which might roll up the open flank of the Allied assault at SWORD. Dropping paratroops behind German lines would also serve to confuse them as to what was the main Allied focus – an airborne invasion or the amphibious assault on the

LEFT Four 'stick' commanders of 22nd Independent Parachute Company, British 6th Airborne Division, synchronizing their watches in front of an Armstrong Whitworth Albemarle at about 23:00 on 5 June 1944, just prior to take-off from RAF Harwell, Oxfordshire. This Pathfinder unit dropped into Normandy in advance of the rest of the division in order to mark out the landing zones, and these men (from left to right, Lieutenants Bobby de la Tour, Don Wells, John Vischer and Bob Midwood) were among the first Allied troops to land in France.

Normandy coast? This would be aided by dropping dummy parachutists called 'Ruperts' to add to German confusion about the Allies' real intent.

Unlike the Americans, who viewed their airborne forces as infantry with parachutes (albeit very good infantry), the British saw theirs as akin to special forces tasked to undertake defined missions. Within this context there were some crucial targets for the

6th Airborne Division. One was the German battery at Merville, which would be assaulted by Lieutenant Colonel Terence Otway's 9th Parachute Battalion (9 Para) with assistance from a company of Canadians. The other was at Pegasus Bridge. A critical part of Allied planning was to deny the Panzers use of the bridges over the River Orne and Canal, forcing them further south to Caen and delaying their ability to launch a cohesive counter-attack. Moreover, from an Allied perspective, this would also support the wider objects of the invasion to hold the crossings that would provide a launchpad for the Allied breakout once the beachheads had been linked up. All of this entailed a coup-de-main assault on Pegasus Bridge, defended by a garrison of around 50 men, mainly drawn from eastern Europe but commanded by German officers and NCOs.

This formidable task fell to three platoons of the Oxfordshire and Buckinghamshire Light Infantry, commanded by Major John Howard. Casting off their tows at 00:07 on 6 June, the pilots of the Glider Regiment managed to land three Horsa Gliders 75 feet (23 metres) from the German defences. Leigh-Mallory called this feat the 'most impressive piece of flying in the war'. The defenders were caught by surprise, allowing Howard's men to take the position in just three minutes. The mortally wounded Lieutenant Den Brotheridge became the first British officer casualty of the invasion. With the bridge in British hands, Howard's men signalled the codeword for success: 'HAM & JAM'.

An initial German counter-attack was beaten off with the only serviceable PIAT before elements of 7 Para under Lieutenant Colonel Pine-Coffin, his bugler sounding a hunting horn, arrived to reinforce Howard's position. By 03:00 Colonel Von Luck's 21st Panzer Division was ready to move but the German higher command would not give him permission until midday, by which time his Panzers provided good targets for Allied airpower. Howard was further bolstered around

13:00 when Commandos under Lord Lovat started to arrive from the SWORD landings. The British 6th Airborne held this vital bridgehead, which was used as part of Operation GOODWOOD, until 18 August and then took part in the breakout from Normandy.

Major John Howard
Company D, 2nd Battalion, Oxfordshire and Buckinghamshire Light Infantry

. . . .

I emerged from the glider, broke my way through all the debris, the wood, which had smashed all around it, and I suppose that really was the most exhilarating moment of my life. Because I stood there and I could see the tower of the bridge about fifty yards from where I was standing. The nose of the glider was right through the German wire-fence, where, back in the UK, I'd almost facetiously asked the glider pilot to put it so we would not have to use Bangalore torpedoes, which every glider had brought with them for the purpose of breaking through the wire. And above all, and this was the tremendous thing, there was no firing at all. In other words, we had complete surprise: we really caught old Jerry with his pants down. But there was no time to wonder about that. I followed the platoon up the track; I saw the smoke bomb explode, the phosphorous bomb; I heard the 'Thud, thud, thud' in the pillbox as the grenades exploded and I knew we'd get no trouble from there.

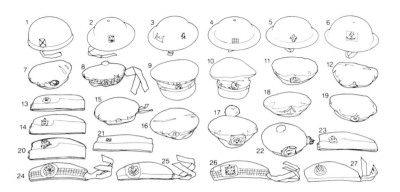

INSIGNIA OF BRITISH AND CANADIAN UNITS

1 Fife and Forfar Yeomanry Tank Regiment

2 Somerset Light Infantry

3 53rd (Welsh) Infantry Division

4 Argyll and Sutherland Highlanders (Canadian)

5 Le Régiment de Maisonneuve (Canadian)

6 Canadian Scottish Regiment

7 Duke of Cornwall's Light Infantry

8 Lovat Scouts

9 Royal Corps of Military Police

10 Officer Royal Canadian Artillery

11 Le Régiment de la Chaudiére (Canadian)

12 Duke of York's Royal Canadian 23rd Hussars

13 Officer Royal Engineers

14 Officer Intelligence Corps

15 4th County of London Yeomanry (Sharpshooters)

16 Green Howards

17 North Nova Scotia Regiment (Canadian)

18 Royal Canadian Artillery

19 Royal Regiment of Canada

20 2nd (Queen's Royal) Regiment of Foot

21 Staffordshire Yeomanry

22 Argyll and Sutherland Highlanders (Canadian)

23 Royal Regiment of Canada

24 Argyll and Sutherland Highlanders

25 Highland Light Infantry

26 Canadian Scottish Regiment

27 Queen's Own Cameron Highlanders of Canada

LEFT Memorabilia of Major Howard, clockwise, from top left: compass, helmet with sniper's bullethole received on 7 June, divisional and regimental insignia, escape and evasion kit issued to all airborne personnel, and (background) a silk escape map of France.

ABOVE When dropped over occupied France this type of quarter-size dummy parachutist, known as a 'Rupert', was intended to sow confusion and carried with it two types of gunfire simulator. Ruperts were dropped by the thousand across northern France during Operation TITANIC to coincide with the real airborne drop.

THE BRITISH AND CANADIAN BEACHES | 85

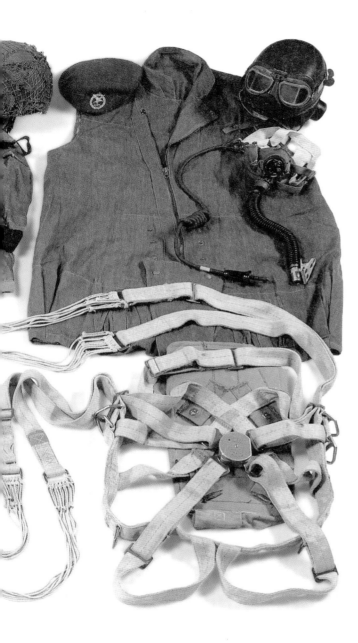
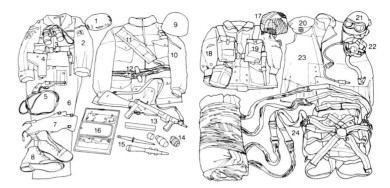

BRITISH AIRBORNE UNIFORMS AND EQUIPMENT

1 Distinctive 'red' beret and cap badge of The Parachute Regiment

2 Pattern 1940 serge battle dress blouse

3 Binoculars

4 Pattern 1937 web waist belt, web ammunition pouch, web holster plus No. 4 bayonet and scabbard with frog

5 No. 2 Mk. I Webley .38in calibre revolver with lanyard

6 Battle dress trousers

7 Pattern 1937 web gaiters

8 'Ammunition' boots (not jump boots)

9 Airborne pattern steel helmet with netting and chin strap

10 Officer's Denison smock

11 Ammunition bandolier for .303in calibre

12 Toggle rope carried by assault troops – each section could be linked with others (using the toggles and loops) to create a scaling rope

13 Sten Mk. III 9mm submachine gun with clip (below the gun)

14 Offensive plastic concussion grenade No. 69 (left) and Mills No. 36 fragmentation grenade (right)

15 Fairbairn-Sykes fighting knife with sheath

16 Folding map case

17 Late pattern airborne helmet with camouflage net and scrim attached

18 Denison smock for other ranks (introduced 1941)

19 Pattern 1937 webbing, ammunition pouches and water bottle

20 Maroon beret with cap badge insignia of the Glider Pilot Regiment

21 Glider pilot's Type C flying helmet

22 Oxygen mask for the Type C helmet

23 Parachute smock used during drops and taken off after landing, worn over the Denison smock and battle dress and under the parachute harness

24 British X-Type parachute

GOLD BEACH

G OLD beach was the middle Allied beach, and at the western end of its 10-mile (16-kilometre) expanse the Allies planned to build MULBERRY B. The 50th Northumbrian Division would land two brigades abreast. The 231st Brigade would land near Le Hamel in the western sector (called Jig) led by the 1st Battalion, the Hampshire Regiment and the 1st Battalion, the Dorset Regiment, with the 2nd Battalion, the Devonshire Regiment forming the follow-up wave. In the eastern sector (King), the 69th Brigade would land near La Rivière, with the 6th Green Howards and the 5th Battalion, the East Yorkshire Regiment in the initial assault, backed up by the 7th Green Howards. 47 Royal Marine (RM) Commando would land behind the 231st and push west, avoiding contact with the enemy, to head with all speed for the harbour at Port-en-Bessin where PLUTO was to be located, before acting as the link-up unit with American forces from OMAHA.

'We had been told, unofficially, that our casualties would be eighty per cent.'

Sergeant John Clegg, Centaur Tank, 1st Royal Marine Armoured Support Regiment

GOLD BEACH FACT FILE

OBJECT	To capture Bayeux and establish a position across RN 13 and ensure liaison with flanking divisions.
NAVAL FORCE	'G' Commodore C.E. Douglas-Pennant on HMS *Bulolo*.
ASSAULT FORCE	50th Northumbrian Division (XXX Corps), Major General D.A.H. Graham.
LANDING TIME	07:25

05:35	Task Force G arrives 7 miles (11 kilometres) off GOLD.
05:45	Preliminary air and naval bombardment commences, lasting 90 minutes.
06:05	Longues *Kriegsmarine* battery opens fire on Task Force G.
07:25	The 231st and 69th Brigades hit the beach and DD tanks are landed.
08.20	Reserve battalions of the initial waves land while the assault wave begins to move inland.
09:30	47 RM Commando lands.
09:50	47 RM Commando skirts around *WN*37 and heads for Port-en-Bessin.
10:50	Reserve brigades start landing.
13:45	Concerted attack on *WN*37 fails.
15:00	69th Brigade engages the enemy at Villers le Sec.
16:00	*WN*37 is finally silenced as the 231st Brigade heads for Arromanches.
19:00	Longues battery finally silenced; it is taken on D+1.
20:30	The 56th and 151st Brigades reach the outskirts of Bayeux.
21:00	Arromanches is captured by 231st Brigade.
24:00	25,000 troops have been landed on GOLD with only 415 casualties. The 50th Northumbrian Division has created a substantial beachhead and linked up with the Canadians at JUNO; 47 RM Commando is in position to seize Port-en-Bessin.

GOLD beach marked the command division between the 716th German Infantry Division, with its 441st Ost Battalion tasked with defending the beach itself, and the 352nd Infantry Division to the west. This Ost Battalion, so the British found out, was made up of many men drawn from the southern parts of the Soviet Union who had been conscripted into German service. The beach obstacles at GOLD consisted of the usual mix of underwater poles with Teller mines and 'hedgehogs' above the high-tide mark. German strongpoints were located in the west at Arromanches, comprising *WN*39, containing a casemated 75mm gun enfilading the beach; *WN*38 with two casemated 50mm guns; and, just inland, *WN*40. In the east, *WN*33 (casemated 88mm in enfilade and two 50mm in casemates) and *WN*34 were located at La Rivière. Between these two strongpoints were three more *WN*s, including a casemated 75mm at Le Hamel in *WN*37. The Germans had disguised some of their defences as pre-war beach kiosks. Inland of King was the Mont Fleury battery (*WN*35a) of four casemated 122mm guns and a mobile battery of four 100mm guns. Along with the heavy guns was the ever-effective combination of minefields, MG42 nests and mortars. Behind the landing zones was a thin stretch of flooded ground.

Between Arromanches and OMAHA beach was the *Kriegsmarine* battery at Longues containing four 150mm naval guns, taken out of destroyers and mounted in concrete casemates with a range out to 23,125 yards (19,500 metres), bringing the landings at GOLD and OMAHA both into range. The Longues Battery, sited about 380 yards (350 metres) back from the cliff-face, could not be observed from the sea and so could not be targeted directly. The battery was garrisoned by 184 *Kriegsmarine* sailors and protected by minefields, barbed wire, 20mm guns and mortars.

Private Kerslake
2nd Battalion, Devonshire Regiment

• •

We attacked one of the gun bunkers [of Longues battery on D+1], where we had to go round to the front as we couldn't make any impression on the heavy door at the back. As we went around the mounds of earth, we came under fire from a very heavy calibre machine gun and only survived as there were plenty of craters from the near misses to hide in.

After my experience of the landing the day before, I was not looking forward to clearing the gun bunker and, even though it was hot, I was in a cold sweat. Under covering fire we went in. After the bright daylight, we couldn't see anything. There were shots that dangerously ricocheted off the walls. I never did find out if they were ours or theirs. We went through the bunker; we had been warned not to use grenades, as we would have in normal buildings, as we could have exploded ammunitions and ourselves with it. We reached the back door and opened it and I nearly got shot by a very young lad from our platoon who was on his own; very jumpy and very white.

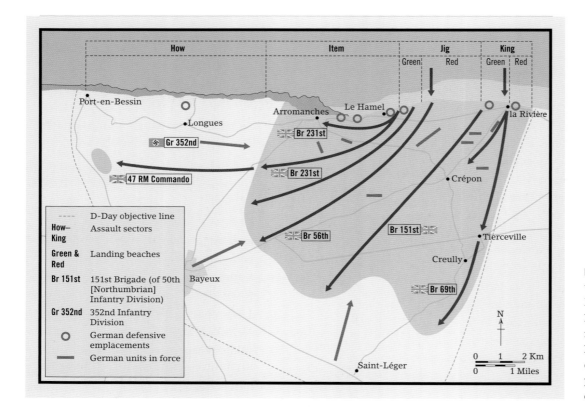

How | **Item** | **Jig** | **King**

Green | Red | Green | Red

Port-en-Bessin
Longues
Arromanches
Le Hamel
la Rivière
Gr 352nd
Br 231st
47 RM Commando
Br 231st
Crépon
Br 56th
Br 151st
Tierceville
Creully
Bayeux
Br 69th
N
Saint-Léger

--- D-Day objective line
How–King Assault sectors
Green & Red Landing beaches
Br 151st 151st Brigade (of 50th [Northumbrian] Infantry Division)
Gr 352nd 352nd Infantry Division
○ German defensive emplacements
▬ German units in force

0   1   2 Km
0   1 Miles

LEFT GOLD beach, showing the assault of the 50th Northumbrian Division and how close the division came to meeting its objective of taking Bayeux. Note the movement of 47 RM Commando to be in position to take Port-en-Bessin on D+1.

The battery was a crucial Allied concern, given the need to build MULBERRY harbours at both of those beaches. On 6 June shells from the battery straddled Task Force G's command vessel HMS *Bulolo*, carrying Lieutenant General Bucknall, commander of XXX Corps and 47 RM Commando. Despite its obvious threat to the landings, Longues Battery would not be assaulted in the same way that Pointe du Hoc was to the west. Instead, air and naval bombardment would be used to reduce its effectiveness, with 6-inch shells from HMS *Ajax* knocking out two of the casemated guns while disabling the remaining two. Accuracy was helped by prior knowledge of the gun battery obtained by the French Resistance and, on 6 June, RAF spotter planes reporting on the fall of shot. However, the battery was not seized until the morning of D+1 when the 2nd Devons, advancing from GOLD and supported by armour, delivered the coup-de-grace, taking 120 prisoners.

As with the American beaches, the weather on 6 June caused some problems. At GOLD the heavy sea state prevented the launching of DD tanks, which were supposed to lead the assault; instead they landed around five minutes after the infantry and the first wave of Hobart's 'funnies', leading to a pile up of men and armour on the beach – 'quite a shambles' according to Major Peter Selerie of the Sherwood Rangers Yeomanry. Yet, the principal beachmaster for GOLD, Lieutenant Commander B.T. Whinney, found that the German beach obstacles 'were not as numerous as I had been led to believe'. At Jig the Dorsets and Hampshires found that the current had shifted them further east than their intended landing areas, with enfilade fire from WN37 contributing further to this drift of the assault wave. They also found that while the preliminary bombardment might have been spectacular to watch, it had not been effective in knocking out German Widerstandnest.

Adding to their woes, as they waded ashore the Hampshires were met by a hail fire from WN36 at the Customs House. Having lost three Sherman DD tanks in the run to the shore, the Sherwood Rangers of the 8th Armoured Brigade lost three more to German fire. Unable to move forward, due to the heavy fire and uncut wire, or along the beach, due to fire from WN37, which accounted for a number of British tanks and AVREs, the Hampshires were pinned down. With radios damaged and the battalion commanding officer, the second in command and the artillery support

'So he fired again and, would you believe, the next one was kind enough to go right in …'

Sergeant Robert Palmer, Essex Yeomanry, 147th Field Regiment Royal Artillery

officer all casualties, there was no way to call in naval gun support. The Hampshires eventually undertook a flanking movement to skirt around WN36 before silencing the bunker.

The Dorsets had also been pushed to the east, but avoided the fate of their colleagues by missing their intended target, WN36, and so got off the beach relatively quickly before starting to move west, wisely going round WN37. This Widerstandnest caused further problems for the 2nd Devons and 47 RM Commando in the follow-up wave. The latter had already suffered particularly badly during the run in to the shore as the rising tide hid mines and 47 RM Commando lost several craft, 43 men and much equipment. The deadly 75mm gun was eventually neutralised by Sergeant Robert Palmer of the Essex Yeomanry. Manoeuvring his 25-pounder Sexton self-propelled gun, from 300 yards (274 metres) his gun layer put a shell through the gun aperture – an action for which he was awarded the Military Medal. However, resistance from machine-gun nests at Le Hamel, and from snipers in a fortified former sanatorium, was not completely overcome until between 15:30 and 16:00.

ABOVE Overhead views of GOLD show the empty landing craft along the beach at Asnelles, taken at approximately 13:00 on 6 June when the tide was again high. Many other vehicles are on the beach and others are moving inland along the roads.

To the east the landings of the 69th Brigade at King sector bore some similarities to the experience of 231st Brigade. With the 5th East Yorkshires and the 6th Green Howards leading the assault, backed up by DD tanks of the 4th/7th Royal Dragoon Guards, further support came from the crab tanks of the Westminster Dragoons of 79th Armoured Division and AVREs of 81st Squadron 6th Assault Regiment. The 88mm gun enfilading the beach from *WN*33 knocked out a number of tanks. Trooper Roland Mole of the 4th/7th Royal Dragoon Guards recalled seeing a Churchill AVRE moving up the beach then 'suddenly there was a flash and sixty tons of metal just disappeared in front of our eyes'.

A shell fired through the gun aperture of *WN*33 by Captain R.F. Bell's Sherman flail tank of the Westminster Dragoons silenced the 88mm.

Taking out the anti-tank guns allowed the various 'funnies' to get on with their obstacle-clearing, providing routes through German wire and minefields for the infantry to begin to move off the beach. The assault on La Rivière itself was led by an AVRE equipped with a mortar firing a 40-pound petard demolition charge, which looked like a flying dustbin. Again, tanks dealt with German positions with supporting infantry clearing out the defenders. 'All you see is the figure of a man in an enemy uniform', according to Private Dennis Bowen of the 5th East Yorkshires; 'you just blindly fire in his direction. And as soon as the magazine is empty, reload and continue firing…. Just keep banging away'. Defenders in the strongpoints started to surrender – and as Sergeant

Neville Howell of the 73rd Anti-Tank Regiment pointed out, many were not actually Germans, 'They looked like Mongolians to me'.

With troops moving inland, the next major obstacle was the Mont Fleury battery. Here, the actions of Company Sergeant Major Stanley Hollis are described best by his Victoria Cross citation (see box, right), the only VC awarded on D-Day. Hollis himself downplayed his actions, arguing: '...that sort of thing was happening all over in the first five days in Normandy....when you saw lads you knew dropping dead, you wanted to do something to smash the guns that had done it'. 'I've sometimes heard that chaps who get medals inspire the other men,' Hollis humbly stated, 'It wasn't like that in my case. My officers and men, they inspire me'.

Despite a problematic start for the initial wave at GOLD, largely caused by the sea state and the German defences at *WN*33 and *WN*37, the reserve 56th and 151st Brigades as well as the remaining units of the 8th Armoured Brigade landed. By the end of D-Day the 50th Division was around a mile short of Bayeux, so it had just fallen short of its objectives – but 25,000 troops had been landed, a beachhead of 5 square miles (13 square kilometres) established and a link-up with the Canadians at JUNO formed. To the west 47 Commando had reached the high ground above Port-en-Bessin, which it would seize the next day. The successful landing and beachhead at GOLD had drawn German focus away from OMAHA, but that raised the question: where were the Americans?

Company Sergeant Major (CSM) Stanley Hollis VC

6th Battalion, Green Howards

● ●

... CSM Hollis instantly rushed straight at the pillbox, firing his Sten gun. He jumped on top of the pillbox, recharged his magazine, threw a grenade in through the door and fired his Sten gun into it killing two Germans and making the remainder prisoner. He then cleared several Germans from a neighbouring trench. ...

Later the same day in the village of Crepon, the Company encountered a field gun and crew armed with Spandaus at 100 yards range. CSM Hollis was put in command of a party to cover an attack on the gun, but the movement was held up. Seeing this, CSM Hollis pushed right forward to engage the gun with a PIAT from a house at 50 yards range. He was observed by a sniper who fired and grazed his right cheek and at the same moment the gun swung round and fired at point blank range into the house. To avoid the falling masonry CSM Hollis moved his party to an alternative position. ... the gun was destroyed shortly afterwards.

...Wherever the fighting was heaviest CSM Hollis appeared and, in the course of a magnificent day's work, he displayed the utmost gallantry .... It was largely through his heroism and resource that the Company's objectives were gained and casualties were not heavier and by his own bravery he saved the lives of many of his men.

ABOVE Royal Navy (RN) Ensign of a Landing Craft, Tank (Rocket) LCT(R) and a smaller, damaged ensign of RN *LCT 7092*. An annotated bombardment chart from the Eastern Task Force, British Sector, for H-30 and H-Hour (the time for which is given in the secret signal, bottom right) shows the landing beaches and the ships in the covering bombardment groups. The landing craft identification booklets were issued by US Naval Intelligence. The D-Day log is from *LCT 2130* (crew photograph, inset).

LEFT Crew photograph of *LCT 2130*, which sailed with the Western Task Force to the American sector, where she arrived off UTAH at 06:30 but only beached (Victor Green) at 11:20.

LEFT A British 3-in mortar with base plate, bipod with elevating and traversing screw, leather tube cover (on the bipod) and a leather sight case, to the left of the metal box for 3-in mortar ammunition. Of the two projectiles, the right-hand one has had the fuze cap removed.

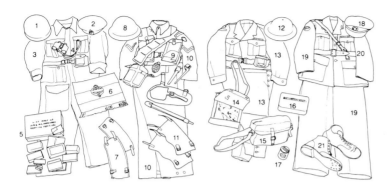

BRITISH ARMY UNIFORMS AND EQUIPMENT

1 Royal Armoured Corps pattern steel helmet

2 Beret with the insignia of the Royal Tank Regiment

3 Armoured crew denim overalls

4 Binoculars and pattern 1937 compass pouch

5 First aid kit for armoured fighting vehicles

6 Royal Tank Regiment designating pennant

7 Pattern 1937 web gaiters dyed black for armoured personnel

8 Mk. III steel helmet

9 Pattern 1937 webbing equipment

10 Battle dress blouse and trousers of a corporal, York and Lancaster Regiment, 146th Brigade, 49th (West Riding) Division

11 Pattern 1937 web gaiter

12 Mk. I steel helmet

13 Battle dress blouse of a major, Royal Engineers, with corduroy (whipcord) jodhpurs

14 Web map case, pattern 1937 web waist belt and compass pouch

15 Web satchel for field signals

16 Tin of chocolates

17 Tin of cigarettes

18 Officer's service dress cap with the insignia of the Royal Engineers

19 Pre-1942 pattern officer's service dress jacket and trousers, bearing insignia of the Royal Engineers, XXX Corps

20 Sam Browne belt

21 Service boots

SMALL ARMS AND ACCOUTREMENTS OF BRITISH, DOMINION AND FREE POLISH FORCES

1 Lee Enfield .303in calibre No. 4 Mk. I (T) sniper rifle with No. 32 sight and lens cap

2 Metal case for the sight

3 Sniper's face veil/scarf

4 Lee Enfield .303in calibre No. 4 Mk. I rifle with flip sight and Mk. I bayonet and scabbard

5 Canvas cover for No. 4 Mk. I rifle

6 Ammunition clips for .303in calibre

7 Lee Enfield .303in calibre No. 4 Mk. I rifle with adjustable sight

8 Water bottle 1937 pattern

9 Enfield No. 2 Mk. I, .38in calibre revolver with web holster

10 Canadian Inglis-Browning No. 1 Mk. I 9mm pistol and holster

11 Webley No. 2 Mk. I, .38in calibre revolver with web holster

12 Enfield No. 2 Mk. I, .38in calibre revolver with armoured crew holster

ABOVE A Sten Mk. II 9mm submachine gun with web bandolier for multiple Sten ammunition clips. Different variations of small arms were made in the USA, Canada, Australia and New Zealand. This Sten gun was made in New Zealand.

JUNO BEACH

J UNO beach comprised a 6-mile (10-kilometre) stretch of the Calvados coastline straddling the small fishing port of Courselles. The coast was populated by small picturesque villages: in the west, JUNO segued into GOLD at La Rivière; the next villages, Vaux and Gray-sur-Mer, were inland and just west of Courselles; Bernières, St. Aubin and Langrune – the latter just beyond the eastern extent of the designated landing zones – were all on the seafront.

Beyond the sand dunes were more villages and hamlets, giving the Germans a network of fortified positions. Along the coast were a number of *Wiederstandnest*: *WN*28 at Bernières had a 50mm gun, anti-tank gun and around a dozen Tobruks; *WN*27 at St. Aubin a 50mm gun and a number of pillboxes; and *WN*26 at Langrune contained a casemated 75mm gun. The real strongpoint was Courselles where several *WN* were grouped together. West of the harbour entrance was *WN*31 with a 75mm gun, two 50mm guns and a number of machine guns and Tobruks; to the east, *WN*29 comprised a casemated 88mm gun, two casemated 75mm guns and six Tobruks. Overlooking the town were machine-gun nests. Inland a mobile battery of four 105mm guns could range in on the beaches, while around 3 miles (5 kilometres) to the

JUNO BEACH FACT FILE

OBJECT	Establish a bridgehead 11 miles (18 kilometres) deep, seizing the heights west of Caen around Carpiquet airfield; 48 Royal Marine Commando to protect the east flank by capturing Langrune-sur-Mer and link up with SWORD.
NAVAL FORCE	'J' Commodore G.N. Oliver on HMS *Hilary*.
ASSAULT FORCE	3rd (Canadian) Division (I Corps), Major General R.F.L. Keller.
LANDING TIME	07:45 7th Brigade, 07:55 8th Brigade.

• •

05:30	Preliminary bombardment.
07:49–08:10	Assault waves hit the beach to stiff resistance.
08:11	DD tanks and AVREs start to land after the infantry.
08:30	Reserve units begin to land but on a rising tide, beach clearance is very difficult. The narrow beach is becoming congested and is under heavy fire; 48 RM Commando lands at St Aubin.
09:00	8th Brigade takes Bernières.
10:40	Five beach exits have been opened by blowing open the seawall.
10:50	Follow-up 9th Brigade starts to land at Bernières.
12:00	Langrune is captured but *WN*26 holds out.
14:00	3rd Division is pushing inland and has linked up with GOLD.
20:00	At Villons-les-Buissons, the North Nova Scotia Regiment encounters stiff resistance and is given orders to dig in.
24:00	21,400 troops are ashore for 915 casualties and some deep-penetrations have been made into the German defence. The link-up with GOLD has been achieved but the failure to link up with SWORD has left 3rd Division's flank open.

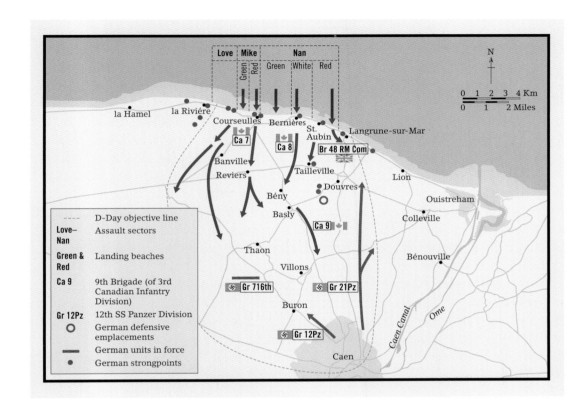

Legend:

- – – – D-Day objective line
- **Love–Nan** Assault sectors
- **Green & Red** Landing beaches
- **Ca 9** 9th Brigade (of 3rd Canadian Infantry Division)
- **Gr 12Pz** 12th SS Panzer Division
- ○ German defensive emplacements
- ▬ German units in force
- • German strongpoints

LEFT JUNO beach and the landing of the 3rd Canadian Division. Note the major point of German resistance at Douvres radar station and the move by 48 RM Commando to try and link up with SWORD to the east. Also, note the German counter-attack by 21st Panzer Division into the gap between JUNO and SWORD.

southeast of Courselles was the German radar station at Douvres, comprising two mutually supporting strongpoints. The front-line defences were manned by around 400 soldiers of the 441st Ost Battalion, 716th Infantry Division, with elements of the 2nd Battalion, 736th Regiment, which also covered SWORD and the British airborne landing zones. Finally, while these defences held up the initial assault, 21st Panzer Division would provide the mobile counter-attack.

Assaulting JUNO on 6 June would be the 3rd Canadian Division under Major General Rod Keller. The plan was, like GOLD, for a two-brigade infantry assault spearheaded by DD Sherman tanks. The naval force had been split into two subsidiary forces. In the west 'J1' carried the 7th Brigade to its designated landing zones, where the Royal Winnipeg Rifles would land at Mike Green and the Regina Rifles at Mike Red. This sector marked the boundary between the two

'People were running up the beach. A few dead bodies. Craft all over the place. Proper mayhem it was.'

Corporal Thomas Stuffling, Royal Marine and LCA Stoker

landing zones, which straddled the entrance to the harbour at Courselles. The 8th Brigade's Queen's Own Rifles of Canada would land at Nan White with the North Shore Regiment at Nan Red. In reserve was the 9th Brigade, ready to support the initial assault wave. In the original COSSAC plan JUNO would have been the easternmost beach, and would have left an open flank for a German counter-attack. It was imperative that the Canadians joined up quickly with the British forces landing to the east at SWORD, and implementing that link-up was the task of 48 Royal Marine Commando, which would land at Nan Red. In total 15,000 Canadians and 9,000 British troops were scheduled to land.

One of the unique aspects at JUNO was a number of apparent offshore reefs which had been picked up by photo reconnaissance (many were actually seaweed). At the other beaches the initial wave was landed on a rising tide, but below the line of beach obstacles before they became submerged and more dangerous. The reefs prevented this at JUNO, so landings would be delayed by a few minutes – the 7th Brigade hitting the beach at 07:45 and the 8th Brigade another 10 minutes behind. In fact, with the Naval Task Force buffeted by bad weather, the landings were further delayed. J.H. Hamilton of the Royal Winnipeg Rifles saw his unit's first casualty, Rifleman Andrew Munch, washed overboard, 'he went down. We never saw him again'. Landing craft beached among the obstacles – a risky process, but one which could not be avoided. The sea state also prevented the launching of the DD tanks so the infantry would have to go in first. The heavy swell and the current pushed landing craft about, causing the formation to lose some cohesion as it approached JUNO. One benefit was that this provided more time for the preparatory bombardment, though it failed to knock out many of the heavier German guns.

On Mike the men of the Royal Winnipeg Rifles landed at 07:49, without any of their supporting DD Shermans or AVREs, where they endured a torrid time. It was a difficult landing, and some of the LCAs became marooned on the rising tide and were sitting targets for German guns. At JUNO just under a third of the landing craft would be destroyed or damaged by mines and beach obstacles, including 29 per cent of the LCAs. Company B lost 20 men coming ashore and a further 100 clearing the German positions; by the time it moved inland it was reduced to just one officer and 25 men. Company D assaulted the concrete casemates of WN31, finally supported by seven DD tanks of the 1st Hussars. Both companies neutralised their respective German coastal emplacements before moving inland. Getting armour off the beach was more problematic as exits remained blocked, and it was not until 09:15 that an exit off Mike beach was opened up by placing a bridge across the top of an AVRE stranded in a crater.

The Regina Rifles had been training for months for their specialist task of clearing Courselles. The Rifles' first wave landed across the harbour on Nan Green and ran straight into *WN*29 but, crucially, 14 DD tanks of the Canadian 6th Armoured Regiment had made it ashore just before the infantry landed at 08:10. With Company A pinned, seeking shelter under the German arcs of fire, men of Company B scurried across the beach under intense fire and entered Courselles. All of the German positions here were eventually knocked out by direct hits from either DD tanks, AVREs or Royal Marine Centaur tanks. Once they fell silent, the German heavy batteries inland started shelling the beach. In the follow-up wave, Company C went straight into sniper-infested Courselles, but Company D's landing craft hit several mines and by the time it assembled ashore it numbered only 49 men. The rising tide hampered the landing of the 9th Brigade as JUNO beach became a compressed mass of men and material, but with Mike and Nan beaches linked up by 12:00, the beach exits open and troops pushing inland, the northern half of Courselles was in Allied hands.

Further east, 8th Brigade's Queen's Own Rifles of Canada landed at Bernières in advance of its armour and under fire from *WN*28 it took heavy casualties in a 200-yard (180-metre) dash for the cover of the seawall. There, German bunkers were cleared the hard way, with grenades and small arms, and after 15 minutes' hard fighting support began to arrive in successive infantry waves. The beach here was cleared of German defenders, but not obstacles, before the armour landed. By mid-morning Bernières was in Canadian hands.

J.H. Hamilton
Royal Winnipeg Rifles

• •

I got off the landing craft and crossed the narrow sandy beach to the edge of the beach sand dune. I got some protection, but still, I suffered a piece of shrapnel lodged in my right nostril. I was unconscious for some time, and being one of the early waves on the beach, there was no first aid station. When I came to, I tried to put one of our field dressings on, but it's pretty hard to dress your own face wound, so I just continued to let it bleed…

When we came off the narrow sandy beach, I saw a number of Canadian-Scottish that had been killed. They were laying about and the red poppies were in bloom then. It struck me then of a poem that we learned in school by Colonel McCrae: 'In Flanders fields the poppies blow/ Between the crosses, row on row'. That certainly struck me, seeing the Canadian-Scottish laying dead amongst the red poppies blowing in the wind.

At 08:00 the North Shore Regiment had landed and attacked German positions at St. Aubin, but it took until 11:15 for an AVRE to silence the troublesome WN27 with a 40-pound petard. The Germans had also fortified the seaside houses, the upper floors of which provided perfect fields of fire for snipers. AVRE petards were used to deal with them by simply demolishing the houses. Now the regiment could start to push inland, meeting stiff resistance at the village of Tailleville, which was not taken until later that afternoon.

Landing in the wake of the North Shore, in a sector of Nan Red not fully cleared of defenders, 48 Royal Marine Commando paid a heavy price, losing two landing craft to mines and suffering heavy casualties. Marine Sam

Sergeant Keith Briggs

Landing Craft Obstacle Clearance Unit

• •

Whilst we were working in the water it was mostly sniper fire with the occasional mortar landing in the sea around us but it didn't do us too much harm. Snipers were our biggest problem. German snipers in the houses above us were sniping all the time. It didn't frighten us so that we couldn't carry out our work. We weren't frightened to death. We carried on and did our job. We knew we had a job to do.

Earl was offered a cigarette by a man next to him, 'I took one and I looked about and then he weren't there any more. He was dead. He'd got one in the side of his head'. Just off the beach Earl found a knocked-out Canadian tank: 'One chap ... was stood there crying. That was all his mates in there, he said. They was all dead in there.' Once off the beach 48 Commando moved towards its object of Langrune led by the formidable Colonel Moulton, but with only 223 out of the 500 marines who had embarked the previous day. In heavy streetfighting they faced WN26, undamaged, and which, despite the best efforts of the Royal Marines and their supporting Centaur tanks, continued to hold out until D+1.

By the end of D-Day the 3rd Canadian Division had landed 21,500 men for around 925 losses, the second-highest beach casualty figure behind the slaughter on OMAHA. The 3rd Division had successfully linked up with GOLD beach in the west and its tanks had made it to the Caen–Bayeux road. But this was at the furthest penetration of the German defences and most of the division was lagging behind. Carpiquet airfield was still in German hands – but more worrying was the failure to take WN26, for by the end of D-Day there was no link-up with SWORD beach. This 2-mile (3-kilometre) gap also included the fortified Douvres radar station.

RIGHT Canadian soldiers from the 9th Brigade's Stormont Dundas & Glengarry Highlanders, coming ashore in the second wave with bicycles onto Nan White near Bernières-sur-Mer. In landing LCI(L) 299 hit a mine on its port side and was badly damaged.

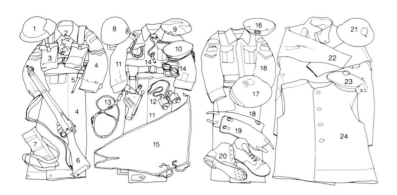

CANADIAN UNIFORMS AND EQUIPMENT

1 Mk. I helmet with netting and field dressing

2 Camouflage scarf

3 Pattern 1937 webbing

4 Battle dress blouse and trousers 'Cameron Highlanders of Ottawa'

5 No. 4 Mk. II bayonet and scabbard

6 No. 4 rifle

7 Ammunition bandolier

8 Armoured corps pattern helmet

9 Beret with insignia of Royal Canadian Transport Corps

10 Denim fatigue beret

11 Battle dress blouse and trousers, major, 4th Armoured Division

12 No. 2 Mk. II binoculars

13 Enfield No. 2 Mk. II, .38in calibre revolver in pattern 1937 holster

14 Mk. III compass with belt pouch and officer's whistle

15 Nylon vehicle aircraft-recognition panel used by the 3rd Canadian Division during Operation TRACTABLE

16 Service cap, Le Régiment de la Chaudiére (Canadian)

17 Mk. III helmet

18 Battle dress blouse and trousers, Le Régiment de la Chaudiére (Canadian)

19 Pattern 1937 web gaiters

20 Steel-reinforced boots

21 Mk. III helmet with insignia of the Black Watch of Canada

22 Oil cloth raincoat

23 Balmoral bonnet of the Black Watch of Canada

24 Leather jerkin

ABOVE By June 1944, 100 of the RAF's 487 squadrons were manned by men from the Commonwealth, who wore these national insignia and squadron badges, from left to right: South Africa (27 squadrons), Rhodesia (one), Australia (16) and New Zealand (six). Canada provided 42 squadrons and India nine.

LEFT The RAF also mustered 31 squadrons from other Allied air forces in Europe – this is a British-made Czech pilot's badge.

RIGHT Poles formed the largest contingent of Allied airmen from continental Europe, with 12 Polish squadrons based in Britain and some personnel serving in RAF squadrons.

LEFT German sniping firearms and accessories, from top to bottom: Karabiner 98k, with muzzle cover, early Waffen-SS rail mount and Ajack 4× sight; Mauser K98k with Czech sight; Gustloff Werke K98k with Dialytan 4× sight and 7.98mm ammunition; Berlin-Lubecker Maschinenfabrik K98k with Zielfernrohr 41 (ZF41) 1.5× sight and (below) carrying case; and a Walther Gewehr 43 (G43) semi-automatic rifle with Gewehr- Zielfernrohr (ZF4) 4× scope, G43 magazine pouches and (right) ZF4 scope and case.

ABOVE From top to bottom: Gustloff Werke K98k with Kahles 4× sight and a sheet metal rail cover and windage wrench; Mauser K98k; Gustloff Werke K98k with Czech 4× scope and case; and a Mauser K98k with an Ajack 4× scope and three sniper's badges instituted in August 1944 – (from the left) 3rd, 2nd and 1st Class kills indicating 20, 40 and 60 confirmed kills.

ABOVE British naval uniforms and equipment, from left to right: Royal Navy captain's service uniform, cap and shoes, with shoulder boards; rating's cap from HMS *Belfast* and a rating's hat with white cover, merchant marine officer's shoulder boards and cap badge; a service wool bridge (duffle) coat with inflatable life belt, bridge binoculars, bosun's whistle and speaking trumpet; and a 'square rig' sailor's dress with a ration tin of Player's Navy Cut cigarettes.

LEFT AND BELOW 'Invasion' francs like these were issued to all Allied troops in France. They were printed in the USA by the Forbes Lithograph Manufacturing Co. of Chelsea, Massachusetts. From 6 June 1944 to 15 June 1945 more than 680 million of these notes were delivered. Legal tender in France, each serviceman on D-Day was issued with 200 francs.

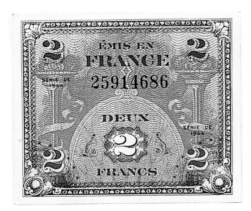

SWORD BEACH

N ine miles (15 kilometres) to the north of Montgomery's principal D-Day object of Caen was the final beach at SWORD. It stretched from Lion-sur-Mer in the west to the mouth of the River Orne, the canal and the city of Ouistreham. The low-lying coastal area was largely featureless, but the 5-mile (8-kilometre) sandy expanse was a pre-war tourist destination and villas and houses lined the seafront.

Along with the usual beach obstacles, mines and anti-tank ditches, the Germans had constructed a number of strongpoints among the coastal villages. From west to east, at Lion-sur-Mer were two casemated 50mm guns in *WN*21, codenamed Trout by the British. *WN*20, known as Cod, was to the east of La Brèche and it housed two casemated 50mm guns and a formidable casemated 88mm. At Ouistreham were two strongpoints that made up *WN*18: at the Casino 'B' contained 50mm and 75mm casemated guns with six machine guns, while 'A' at Riva-Bella had six 155mm heavy guns in open emplacements. To the rear of Ouistreham were *WN*14 (Sole), the headquarters of the 1st Battalion of the 736th Infantry Regiment, and *WN*12 (Daimler) with four casemated 155mm guns. A little further inland on the high ground of the Periers Ridge, on the crucial road to Caen, were *WN*16 (Morris, with four casemated

SWORD BEACH FACT FILE

OBJECT	To capture Caen as soon as possible and link up with 6th (British) Airborne Division.
NAVAL FORCE	'S', Rear-Admiral A.G. Talbot, on HMS *Largs*.
ASSAULT FORCE	3rd (British) Infantry Division, (I Corps), Major General T.G. Rennie.
LANDING TIME	07:25

● ●

06:00	LCAs launched from the larger ships.
07:25	First wave hits the beach.
07:50	1st Special Service Brigade of No. 4 and No. 10 (Free French) Commandos land.
08:35	Three beach exits are clear.
09:00	Hermanville is taken.
09:30	With a rising tide, the beach is becoming cluttered; Royal Navy Beachmasters have difficulty getting vehicles off the beach.
12:00	By midday German positions inland are taken.
13:30	Lovat's Commandos link up with the 6th Airborne at Pegasus Bridge.
16:00	Counter-attack by 21st Panzer Division develops.
20:15	Hillman is finally subdued.
21:00	Elements of 21st Panzer, which have reached Lion-sur-Mer, begin to retreat as Allied gliderborne troops come to reinforce 6th Airborne.
24:00	29,000 troops had been landed on SWORD Beach, with 630 casualties. But British troops are still 3 miles (5 kilometres) short of Caen.

'... get off my bloody beach.'

Royal Navy beachmaster to Corporal Patrick Hennesey, Sherman tank commander, 13th/18th Hussars

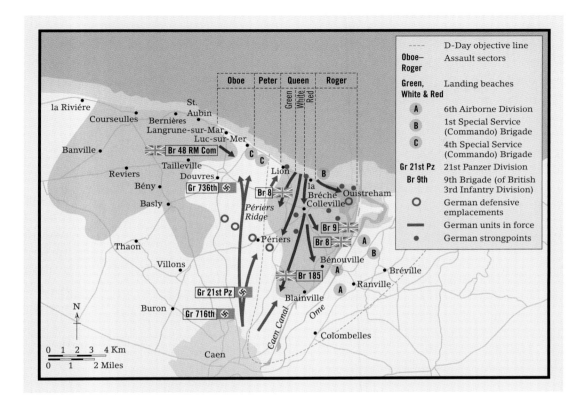

Map legend:

- - - -	D-Day objective line
Oboe– Roger	Assault sectors
Green, White & Red	Landing beaches
Ⓐ	6th Airborne Division
Ⓑ	1st Special Service (Commando) Brigade
Ⓒ	4th Special Service (Commando) Brigade
Gr 21st Pz	21st Panzer Division
Br 9th	9th Brigade (of British 3rd Infantry Division)
O	German defensive emplacements
▬	German units in force
•	German strongpoints

LEFT SWORD beach and the landing of the 3rd (British) Infantry Division. Heavy German resistance and the counter-attack from 21st Panzer Division meant that the British attempt to take Caen on 6 June fell short. Note the danger of 21st Panzer Division falling onto the eastern flank and hence the importance of the 6th Airborne Division holding onto the Orne River and Canal crossings.

100mm guns) and *WN*17, the Hillman bunker complex that headquartered the 736th Infantry Regiment. Sited to fire on any naval landing force were the 75mm guns of the Merville Battery, 5 miles (8 kilometres) to the east across the estuary, while the 155mm guns 20 miles (32 kilometres) to the east at Le Havre were within range. All this defensive firepower was designed to hold up an assault before an armoured counter-attack from 21st Panzer, 12th SS Panzer and the Panzer Lehr divisions.

Attacking SWORD would be the 3rd British Infantry Division of Lieutenant General Miles Dempsey's British Second Army. The beach had four sectors: Oboe in the west; Peter, Queen and Roger in the east. Offshore shoals limited the landing to a single brigade width: 8th Brigade would assault Queen White and Queen Red. Due to the lack of navigational features, Operation GAMBIT saw two midget submarines placed off SWORD on 4 June to guide in the invasion flotilla.

The brigade would be led by the DD tanks of the 13th/18th Hussars and the AVREs of 22nd Dragoons, Westminster Dragoons and the 5th Assault Regiment Royal Engineers (RE), all of 79th Armoured Division. The first wave of infantry comprised the 1st Battalion of the South Lancashire Regiment landing at Queen White, which would secure Hermanville and the 2nd Battalion of the East Yorkshire Regiment at Queen Red, which would neutralise Sole and Daimler. They would be followed by the 1st Suffolks with Morris and Hillman as their objectives. Ramps of landing craft would hit the beach at 07:25.

Attached to the 8th Brigade were Commando units to fulfil specialist tasks. The Ouistreham strongpoints would be tackled by 4 Commando, which included two troops of the Free French from 10 Commando under Captain Philippe Keiffer to assault the Casino. To the west 41 Commando would head for Trout. After the initial wave was ashore, Lord Lovat's 1st Special Service Brigade was to move off the beach, pushing inland to relieve the 6th Airborne, holding key points east of the Orne and thereby securing the eastern flank.

With the first wave objectives and the beachhead secured, 185th Brigade would land and move through 8th Brigade onto their ultimate object of Caen. To obtain room for manoeuvre, it was imperative to push the landing force as far inland and beyond the high ground of the Periers Ridge; then to seize Caen. This would prevent the Germans using Caen as a hinge on which to pivot a counter-attack; and, given Caen's importance

as a transport hub, it would provide the Allies with a strong base from which to develop further offensive operations. This was crucial, for the British planners knew that not only was the 21st Panzer Division near Caen but so too was the 12th SS Panzer Division. Together these formations had the ability to throw the 3rd British Division back into the sea.

With NGS, self-propelled guns and rockets creating a mass of smoke to cover the beaches, the DD tanks were dropped out at nearly 3 miles (4,500 metres); 31 out of 40 made it to the beach, either just in advance or mixed in with the infantry. In the choppy sea it was inevitable that some confusion arose and when landing ramps hit the beach at 07:25, LCAs unloaded their men at the same time as AVREs from LCTs while the DD tanks engaged their tracks. The assault wave had, in effect, all landed together and in the jostling for landing positions the men of Company A 1st South Lancs found themselves near strongpoint Cod, which was supposed to be tackled by the 2nd East Yorks. Taking heavy casualties, including their company commander, they shook out and headed for Lion-sur-Mer.

Cod was engaged by Company C and men from the East Yorks, while Company B of the South Lancs also landed near the strongpoint and suffered casualties, including the battalion commander. It took the combined efforts of the companies to work their way around the back of Cod and neutralise it from the rear. At Queen Red, the East Yorks had been taking heavy fire from defensive batteries enfilading the beach, which were engaged by the 13th/18th Hussars, 22nd Dragoons and the Westminster Dragoons. All troops in the initial waves had been told to push off the beach. 'You didn't stop when someone got hit', Private William Lloyd of the East Yorks recalled. 'You didn't stop to see what happened to them. You knew you'd got to get on.' By pushing on, both of the assault wave battalions had started to secure beach exits and had moved inland by 09:00; the South Lancs had taken Hermanville and the East Yorks were heading for strongpoint Sole.

Before Cod had been silenced, and with obstacle-clearance teams operating under fire, the follow-on waves had started to land, including the Commandos of 1st Special Service Brigade and elements of 41 Commando. Under heavy fire, they fought their way off the beaches and began their tasks. Landing at Queen White, 41 Commando cleared Lion-sur-Mer, having found Trout deserted, but after this successful start they became bogged down in fierce fighting around the château to the west, which prevented them pushing further along the coast and linking up with the rest of the 4th Special Service Brigade landing at JUNO. Lovat's 1st Special Service Brigade moved onto the road leading to Ouistreham, where Captain Keiffer's Free French Commandos stormed the German Casino position. Lovat had sent 6 Commando directly to relieve the 6th Airborne holding those vital positions east of the Orne, and the Commandos arrived only two and a half minutes behind schedule with the rest of the 1st Special Service Brigade coming up behind.

By this time the German defenders manning the coastal positions were starting to withdraw and the landing of the 185th Brigade could commence, with the entire brigade ashore by mid-morning. It was not without incident – Sergeant George Rayson of the 1st Suffolks was on an LCA that dropped its ramp in deep water and he was dragged under the craft, before

Piper Bill Millin
Headquarters, 1st Special Service Brigade

• •

Lovat looked round and seen me standing and said, 'Aw, give us a tune'…The whole thing was ridiculous and I thought I might as well be ridiculous as well. I said, 'What tune would you like, sir?' and he said, 'Well, play *The Road to the Isles*.' I said, 'would you like me to march up and down?' and he said, 'Yes, yes, march up and down. That'll be lovely'…the bodies lying in the water were going back and forward with the tide and I started off piping and going a few paces along. And the next thing there's a hand on my shoulder and a voice said, 'Listen, boy,' and I looked round. It was this sergeant I recognised and he says, 'What are you fucking playing at, you mad bastard? You're attracting all the German attention. Every German in France knows we're here now, you silly bastard'. Anyway, I walked away and of course there were other people up on the wall going, 'Hooray!', Cheering, you know.

LEFT Commandos of 1st Special
Service Brigade landing on 6
June from an LCI(S) (Landing
Craft Infantry Small) on Queen
Red, SWORD, at La Breche, at
approximately 08:40. In the
column advancing through the
water, Lord Lovat is to the right.
The man in the foreground is
Piper Bill Millin, whose bagpipes
(see page 122) can be seen
protruding in front of him.

popping up to its rear. Jettisoning all his kit he managed
to swim ashore, where he found his company had
moved on. After tracking them down, he was welcomed
with typical black humour: 'We know what you was
doing. Swimming back. Didn't like the look of France.'

Around 11:00 three battalions were ready at
Hermanville for the advance on Caen, though some of

the armour was stuck in an almighty traffic jam on the
beach (caused in part by the high tide, which left just 30
feet/9 metres of beach onto which troops and vehicles
could be landed). Royal Navy beachmasters were faced
with clearing the traffic and Lieutenant Commander
Edward Gueritz had to close the beach for a short time
in order to bring order to the chaos and get vehicles

moving inland. Things started well and with Morris subjected to NGS, it fell to the 1st Suffolks around 13:00.

It was a completely different matter with Hillman. Its garrison included Colonel Ludwig Krug's 736th Infantry Regiment, all secure in underground bunkers. Hillman had not been subjected to NGS because the Naval Forward Bombardment Officer with the ground troops had been killed. In trying to bypass the strongpoint the 1st Norfolks suffered 150 casualties. Clearly, if the 3rd Infantry Division was to advance on Caen, Hillman must fall. A storming party from the Suffolks got through the barbed wire but, under heavy machine-gun fire, could not clear the minefield. The tank support from the Staffordshire Yeomanry could not penetrate the steel cupolas, which had to be neutralised with demolition charges, which in turn required the clearance of the minefields and for the tanks to get closer. Until early evening the Suffolks were tied up in clearing the site, trench by trench, bunker by bunker. Support later came from the 13th/18th Hussars, but the nitty-gritty work of blowing bunkers was done by hand. As the Suffolks closed in on Krug, he finally surrendered around 20:15. The Suffolks dug in for the night. Hillman might have fallen but Krug had delayed the British advance long enough to save Caen.

While the Suffolks were dealing with Hillman the only real German counter-attack of 6 June had been developing to the west. By 16:00 Lieutenant General Feuchtinger had concentrated 98 tanks of his 21st Panzer Division north of Caen. It had taken him much

of the day, for with the British 6th Airborne holding the River Orne and Canal crossings, he had been prevented from falling onto the flank of SWORD beach. Instead, his armoured thrust to drive the British back into the sea would be directed at the gap between JUNO and SWORD beaches where the resistance of Douvres radar station and Hillman strongpoint provided useful holding actions. At Biéville, the 2nd Battalion, 22nd Panzer Regiment ran straight into the 2nd Battalion, King's Shropshire Light Infantry, halting the latter's advance on Caen but losing eight tanks in the process to anti-tank weapons. To the west, the 1st Battalion of the 22nd Panzer Regiment lost 13 tanks to the Staffordshire Yeomanry's Sherman Fireflies, blunting that part of the German counter-attack. But it was 1st Battalion, 192nd Panzergrenadier Regiment that made the greatest inroads, pushing directly into the open ground between the Allied beaches. By early evening it had reached the sea at Lion-sur-Mer but, isolated from the rest of the division and with further Allied reinforcements arriving, began to withdraw around 21:00.

By the end of 6 June the Allies had landed 29,000 men at SWORD beach for the loss of 630 casualties. German losses were substantially higher, with many taken prisoner. The British had linked up with their isolated Airborne units to present a cohesive flank to the east but, crucially, had not linked up with JUNO. Moreover, although the counter-attack by 21st Panzer Division had failed to stop the landings, it had stopped the Allies a few miles short of their objective: Caen.

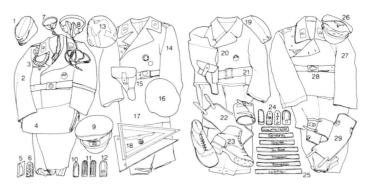

GERMAN ARMOURED UNIT UNIFORMS AND INSIGNIA

1 Officer's field cap with pink Panzer service colour

2 NCO Panzer jacket with cuff title 'Afrika Korps', an entitlement of 21st Panzer Division

3 Panzer marksmanship lanyard

4 Panzer trousers

5 General's collar tab

6 Lieutenant general's shoulder tab

7 Throat microphone

8 Vehicle intercom headphones

9 Officer's cap

10 Major's shoulder strap

11 Pair of lieutenant's shoulder straps

12 NCO's shoulder straps

13 Helmet with cover

14 Self-propelled gun crew NCO's jacket with red artillery service colour

15 Army waist belt and holster for P.38

16 M1943 helmet

17 Self-propelled gun crew trousers

18 General's vehicle pennant, found at the Panzer Group West HQ at Château-la-Caine

19 Waffen-SS Panzer field service cap

20 Waffen-SS Pea pattern camouflage Panzer uniform

21 Pistol belt and Radom P.35p holster

22 Web gaiters for short combat boots

23 Short combat boots

24 Four SS shoulder straps, left to right: major, lieutenant, captain, corporal (1st SS Panzer Division)

25 SS divisional cuff titles, top to bottom: 17th SS Panzer Grenadiers, 10th SS Panzer, 1st SS Panzer, 2nd SS Panzer, 12th SS Panzer, 9th SS Panzer and 1st SS Regiment (part of 2nd SS Panzer)

26 *Luftwaffe* officer's service cap

27 First Lieutenant's Panzer jacket and trousers

28 *Luftwaffe* enlisted man's waist belt

29 *Luftwaffe* web gaiters

MORNING EDITION

HINTON DAILY NEWS

Keep it Flying!

VOLUME XLII. NUMBER 27   HINTON, WEST VIRGINIA TUESDAY AFTERNOON, JUNE 6, 1944   PRICE FOUR CENTS

INVASION BEGINS

Landings Made In Northern France; Nazis Acknowledge Penetrations At Cherbourg

PARA TROOPS LED INVASION

By HOWARD COWAN

WITH UNITED STATES PARACHUTE TROOPS, June 6 (P)—American paratroopers—stubbed with battle-hardened veterans of the Sicilian and Italian campaigns—landed behind Hitler's Atlantic wall today to plant the first blow of the long-awaited second front squarely in the enemy's vitals.

The Allied landing, without benefit of war succeeded from history's boldest stab in an invasion operation.

Two-engined C-47s—sisters of America's standard airliner fleet—bore the human drop across the Allied simultaneously towing through the CG4A gliders to attempt in a single smoothfamous blow paving the way for doomed assault forces.

Armed with weapons from the most primitive to the most modern, the paratroopers' mission was to disrupt and demoralize the German communications lines and lower the power even lines.

There was no immediate indication that their dynamite and flaming steel and steel-speed fire has not succeeded in the execution of plans released by headquarters in preparation for the invasion of occupied Europe.

The awe-inspired, able-to-eyed sacrifice was a real, while also huge are their fact outline in the face and conflicted a less-spirited two hours before daw.

MEADOWS REPORTS $2,700 EXPENSES

CHARLESTON, W. Va., June 6 (P)—Circuit Judge Clarence W. Meadows, Democratic nominee for Governor, reported to the Secretary of State today that he received contributions of $2,700 and had expenses of $2,774 during his primary campaign.

Moore M. Messinger of Parkersburg, Republican nominee for Congress in the Second District, reported $1,000 expenses and in the Panhandle of expenditures of...

WITH BOTH FEET

EISENHOWER TELLS PATRIOTS, 'BE PATIENT, WAIT FOR SIGNAL'

By A.I. GOLDBERG

SUPREME HEADQUARTERS, Allied Expeditionary Force, June 6 (P)—Gen. Dwight D. Eisenhower, the commander of the Allied expeditionary forces, sent to the people of invaded-occupied Europe a message to the peoples of Europe...

INVASION WEATHER

LONDON, June 6 (P)—The sun broke through heavy clouds at Caen in the Dover Strait area this first day of the Allied invasion of western Europe.

After a daybreak shower there was sunshine, but later banks of heavy clouds came up from the northwest. There were further sunny periods, although the outlook was less settled.

The wind blew fairly hard during the night, but lost some of its strength after dawn. A moderate sea was kicked up.

PERSHING ISSUES STATEMENT

INVASION BULLETINS

SUPREME HEADQUARTERS, ALLIED EXPEDITIONARY FORCE, June 6 (P)—United States warships are supporting the Allied landings in France and U. S. Coast guard units also are participating in the operations, it was announced today.

American Marine forces are in the fighting, manning secondary guns aboard the big ships.

LONDON, June 6 (P)—The German radio reported today that four British parachute divisions had landed between Le Havre and Cherbourg to France.

This was first time that the Nazi parachute force dropped on Caen to the Mediterranean.

LONDON, June 6 (P)—The German News Agency gave in a broadcast shortly before 11 a.m. (SAMEWT) that Anglo-American troops had reinforced 31 Havre at the mouth of the Seine river in the Le Havre area.

(By The Associated Press)
The Berlin radio broadcast a DNB dispatch today saying that one Allied cruiser and a large landing vessel carrying troops had been sunk in the area of St. Vaast La Hougue, 15 miles southeast of Cherbourg.

NEW YORK, June 6 (P)—The Berlin radio, in a broadcast recorded by the federal communications commission and said that King George VI would deliver a special broadcast tonight at 9 P. M. London time. (1 P.M.)

NEW YORK, June 6 (P)—The London radio, in a broadcast recorded by NBC, said this morning that strong Allied air attacks have been launched in the Dieppe area.

GENERAL EISENHOWER TELLS TROOPS ONLY FULL VICTORY WILL BE ACCEPTED BY ALLIES

By WES GALLAGHER

SUPREME HEADQUARTERS, Allied Expeditionary Force, June 6 (AP)—Allied forces landed in northern France early today in history's greatest overseas operation, designed to destroy the power of Hitler's Germany and wrest enslaved Europe from the Nazis.

The German radio said the landings were made from Le Havre to Cherbourg, along the north coast of Normandy and the south side of the bay of the Seine.

Allied headquarters did not specify the locations, but left no doubt whatever that the landings were on a gigantic scale.

Ringing in their ears, the American, British and Canadian forces who made the landings had these words from their supreme commander, Gen. Dwight D. Eisenhower:

"You are about to embark on a great crusade. The eyes of the world are upon you and the hopes and prayers of all liberty-loving peoples go with you . . .

"We will accept nothing less than full victory."

The German radio filled the air with invasion flashes for three hours before the formal Allied announcement came at 7:32 a. m. Greenwich Mean Time (3:32 a. m. Eastern War Time).

It acknowledged deep penetrations of the Cherbourg peninsula by Allied parachute and glider troops in great strength.

The assault was supported by gigantic bombardments from Allied warships and planes, which the Germans admitted set the coastal area ablaze.

A senior officer at supreme headquarters said rough water caused "awful anxiety" for the seaborne troops but that the landings were made successfully, although some soldiers were undoubtedly seasick.

The sun broke through heavy clouds periodically this morning after a daybreak shower. The wind had blown fairly hard during the night but moderated with the dawn. The weather outlook remained somewhat unsettled.

Supreme headquarters' first communique was a single sentence:

LEFT Allied newspapers on 6–7 June announce the landings: the *Hinton Daily News* in West Virginia, USA, and the *Daily Telegraph*, *Evening Standard* and *Daily Mirror* in the UK. In Europe, France's *Le Matin* refers to the invaders as 'the enemy', while *Metzer Zeitung* in Germany mentions the unbreakable Atlantic Wall. The resistance news sheet *Free Dane* describes 'joy and expectation all over Denmark'.

PART THREE

THE BREAKOUT

'The battle belonged that morning to the thin, wet line of khaki that dragged itself ashore on the channel coast of France.'

General Omar Bradley

For many men the 24 hours of 6 June 1944 were the most traumatic of their lives. By 24:00 on D-Day the Allies had landed by amphibious assault 75,215 men at GOLD, JUNO and SWORD, 57,500 men at UTAH and OMAHA, and a further 23,000 in the airborne operations. Over 155,000 Allied troops were lodged in France. The day had not been without its problems, most notably in the high losses among the airborne formations and the slaughter at OMAHA, and many D-Day objectives were unfulfilled, but overall the landings were a success. While D-Day was the culmination of over a year's worth of planning, it was just one day at the start of a long process: the liberation of Europe from Nazi tyranny.

The next phase was ensuring the Allies could present a coherent front line, without leaving gaps into which German armour could counter-attack –

as had happened with 21st Panzer. By 8 June all five beaches were linked up and with the fall of Carentan to American forces on 12 June the Allies commanded a 50-mile (80-kilometre) front. There were isolated pockets of resistance, the radar station at Douvres was not subdued until 17 June, but these were now mere hindrances to the Allies rather than major problems.

One priority was to continue with FORTITUDE, leaving the enemy guessing whether this was the real invasion or a diversion for a strike at Pas-de-Calais. On 8 June Agent Garbo continued to draw attention to the fictional FUSAG in southeast England. As late as 3 July (D+24) Colonel General Alfred Jodl, Hitler's operational chief-of-staff could conclude: '… it is obvious that Patton's Army Group (18 infantry, 6 armoured and 5 airborne divisions) is being made ready in London and southern England for the next landing…We conclude

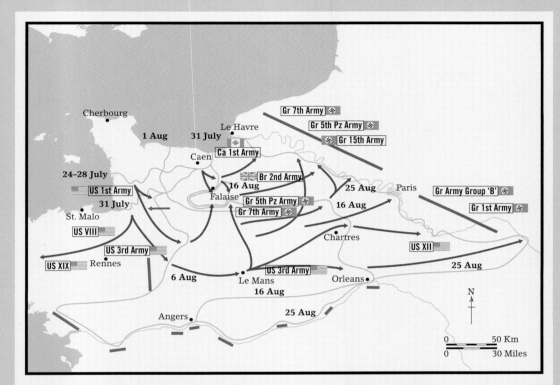

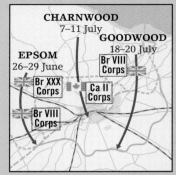

CHARNWOOD
7–11 July
GOODWOOD
18–20 July

EPSOM
26–29 June

Br VIII Corps

Br XXX Corps

Ca II Corps

Br VIII Corps

Cherbourg

1 Aug   31 July
Le Havre
Caen
Ca 1st Army
Gr 7th Army
Gr 5th Pz Army
Gr 15th Army

24–28 July
US 1st Army
31 July
St. Malo
US VIII

16 Aug
Falaise
Br 2nd Army
Gr 5th Pz Army
Gr 7th Army
25 Aug   Paris
16 Aug
Gr Army Group 'B'
Gr 1st Army

US 3rd Army
US XIX   Rennes
Chartres
US XII

6 Aug   Le Mans   Orleans
16 Aug
US 3rd Army
16 Aug
25 Aug

Angers   25 Aug

N

0   50 Km
0   30 Miles

LEFT The Allied Breakout from Normandy. Three operations (inset) were needed to take Caen in the east, which drew in German armour and allowed the Americans to launch Operation COBRA in the west to break out from the *bocage*. Also note the creation of the Falaise pocket.

that the enemy will plan operations with both army groups on both sides of the Seine.' Only 51 days after D-Day, on 27 July, were reinforcements directed from northern France to Normandy.

Keeping the Germans in the dark was integral to the Allies bringing overwhelming force to bear in Normandy and that required a 24/7 logistical operation. Starting on D+1 the varied range of GOOSEBERRIES, BOMBARDONS, PHOENIXES and WHALES arrived

off OMAHA and GOLD beaches to be turned into the MULBERRY harbours. On 14 June, D+8, the first ship was unloaded and by 19 June 24,000 tons per day were being unloaded at the artificial harbours. The Allies had been landing stores directly onto the beaches and this continued while the MULBERRY harbours were in use. On 19 June the weather broke as a storm raged for three days wrecking MULBERRY A at OMAHA and damaging MULBERRY B at Arromanches. Supplies being landed

ABOVE Mulberry B at Arromanches – note the sea state outside the breakwaters compared to the calm inside. Mulberry B was important for six months until after Antwerp was captured.

dropped to 4,500 tons a day, almost all through a repaired MULBERRY B using what could be salvaged from A. By early July MULBERRY B was only handling 7,000 tons per day compared to 10,000 tons landed on the British beaches and 35,000 at OMAHA, where the artificial breakwaters survived the storm. In total around 15 per cent of the Allied stores for the entire campaign came through the MULBERRY harbours.

Was it worth it? Yes. A port had always been a key Allied requirement that needed to be solved in planning for the invasion to be launched, so MULBERRY was crucial to the invasion actually taking place. Moreover, the Allies were still unsure if the Normandy beaches would be suitable for the direct landing of stores, something that could only be found out by actually doing it under the protection of the artificial breakwaters. MULBERRY B was vital for stormy days, providing a safe refuge for Allied shipping and allowing ships to unload when it was impossible to land stores on the beaches. Unloading at a MULBERRY was also faster, 23 minutes for an LST to unload compared with up to 90 minutes at a beach, and of course at the MULBERRY there was no need to wait for the tide to refloat an LST. The main logistical node in Allied planning was Cherbourg, but American forces met stiff resistance when it was assaulted on 22 June and the harbour area was not secured until 30 June. With the Germans wrecking the port facilities at the end of July, Cherbourg could still only handle 3,900 tons a day. The top of the Cotentin Peninsula was, of course, far removed from the bitter fighting at the eastern end of the Allied frontline.

During 1944 and 1945 one of the greatest headaches facing SHAEF was maintaining supply lines. On 15 August the Allies launched Operation DRAGOON, the invasion of the south of France, which opened up further port capacity to the point that around a third of the supplies for the rest of the campaign came through that route. A reliable logistical network was crucial in enabling the Allies to prosecute the war in Europe.

A key factor in the Allied ground campaign in Normandy was overwhelming air superiority. The Germans found it nearly impossible to move their formations in daylight. On 11 June Rommel lamented this difficulty: 'The movement of smaller formations on the battlefield ... artillery going into position, placing of

armoured cars and the like, is ... immediately bombed from the air with annihilating effect.'

In the east, it took three major offensive operations to finally crack the German defence of Caen. Operation EPSOM on 26 June saw VIII Corps push a 5-mile (8-kilometre) salient into the German line before being pushed back by a formidable array of German armour in the form of seven Panzer Divisions: Panzer Lehr, 2nd Panzer, 21st Panzer, 1st SS Panzer, 9th SS Panzer, 10th SS Panzer and 12th SS Panzer. On 7 July, in Operation CHARNWOOD, I Corps attacked the northern part of Caen, following an aerial bombardment during which around 3,000 French civilians were killed. In bitter fighting the 3rd Canadian Division lost more men than on D-Day. It took further fighting in Operation GOODWOOD (18–20 July) for the Germans finally to be pushed out of Caen.

The combat around Caen had been brutal – a costly battle of attrition. The patchwork of high Normandy hedgerows and small fields, known as the *bocage*, with stone farmhouses and numerous small villages, provided excellent defensive terrain. The Germans, many of whom had perfected their skills fighting the Russians on the Eastern front, used their combination of MG42, mortars, mines and Panzerfaust anti-tank weapons to great effect while their armoured formations counter-attacked. The Americans found the *bocage* made for particularly tough going in the west, whereas in the east the problems facing the British and Canadians were compounded by the fact

> ## 'I've fought a lot of people, but if you haven't fought the Germans you don't know what fighting is.'
>
> Lieutenant Colonel Peter Young, 6 Commando

that by late June the Germans had seven armoured formations deployed there but only the equivalent of half an armoured division in the west. On 12 June Tiger tank ace Michael Wittman, with four other Tigers, destroyed the head of a column of the British 22nd Armoured Brigade catching it strung out along a road at Villers-Bocage. In GOODWOOD British VIII Corps had committed 700 tanks and lost 220 by the end of the first day. Fighting in the *bocage* took time for the Allies to get to grips with. Although progress through the *bocage* remained slow, the Allies could replace their losses whereas for the Germans attrition was fatal. Panzer Lehr Division, which had mustered over 8,500 men, had been ground down to just 1,531 only 11 days after D-Day. These were losses that could not be replaced. Despite this, the Germans remained combat effective, particularly the Nazi fanatics in the SS formations.

With the Germans deploying the majority of their armour in the east, the breakthrough for the Allies came in the west. There the Americans were desperate to bring to an end a month of fierce fighting in the *bocage* and break out into the rolling plains where their superior numbers and mobility could be exploited. Apart from the *bocage* the Americans were also faced with the 2nd SS Panzer Division, which had started moving towards Normandy on 8 June but took 17 days to complete its march, delayed by a combination of French Resistance, SOE and Allied air operations. *En route* it committed a number of atrocities. With reinforcements arriving in the west the Germans could not prevent St. Lo falling to the Americans on 17 July. On 25 July the American VII Corps launched Operation COBRA, making remarkable gains and led by the talismanic figure of General Patton.

In early August a German counter-attack around Mortain was devastated by Allied airpower while American ground forces held on. With British and Canadian units pressing down from Caen towards Falaise, a pocket of German resistance started to develop that the Allies began to encircle. On 15 August all German units were ordered to retreat to the east but by then the Allies had shattered the defenders as the German forces in France started to disintegrate. By 18 August, what was left of 20 German divisions – around 100,000 men – were trying to escape the closing jaws of Allied encirclement. As this noose tightened, Polish troops at times resorted to fighting the 2nd SS Panzer Corps with bayonets and their bare hands when their ammunition ran out; escape routes became choked with the bodies of men, horses and the burned-out wreckage of German tanks and vehicles – a mass of flesh, horseflesh and metal which provided ideal targets

for Allied aircraft. At Falaise the Germans lost 10,000 men killed, 50,000 men taken prisoner and around 5,000 armoured vehicles and tanks along with more than 8,000 horses, which were vital for transport given the paucity of German fuel supplies. The German Army was in full retreat, having lost 400,000 men in the Normandy campaign compared to Allied losses of 226,000. By 21 August the Allies could muster some 2,000,000 men in northern France. Four days later, 25 August 1944, Paris was liberated, with the advance spearheaded by a Free French armoured column. D-Day and the battle for Normandy were over.

ABOVE Waffen-SS uniforms, clockwise from the left: camouflage smock and helmet; M1943 field cap and blouse of 30th Waffen-SS Grenadier Division (Russian No. 2); and non-regulation jacket from 1st SS Panzer Division 'Liebstandarte Adolf Hitler' with M1940 helmet and 6×30 binoculars and case.

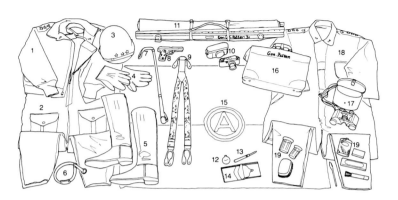

UNIFORMS AND BELONGINGS OF GENERAL GEORGE S. PATTON, JR.

1 Modified winter combat jacket with added epaulets and insignia

2 Modified winter combat trousers with added pockets

3 M1 steel helmet

4 Wool-lined leather gloves (private purchase)

5 Pre-war service cavalry boots, made by Peal & Co., London (private purchase)

6 Dog collar with dog tag 'Willie Patton 02605 K-9, 3rd Army', worn by Patton's bull terrier

7 Leather riding crop

8 Colt .380in calibre automatic

9 Braces from Hammacher Schlemmer, New York (private purchase)

10 German Leica camera and case

11 'Komfort Kot', a folding cot made by Byer Manufacturing Co., Orono, Maine

12 Abercrombie & Fitch pocket watch and alarm (private purchase)

13 Pocket knife

14 Wallet, embossed, made by Mark Cross, London

15 Flag of Third Army

16 Leather briefcase

17 Binoculars with case, marked 'Patton, 15th Cav'

18 Modified herringbone twill work suit with added epaulets and insignia

19 Selection of toiletries (private purchases)

LEFT Two Waffen-SS uniforms worn by personnel of 12th SS Panzer Division 'Hitler Jugend'. On the left an Italian Navy black leather uniform with M43 field cap, Waffen-SS belt and buckle, Radom P.35 holster and short laced boots. On the right a jacket and trousers in Italian camouflage known as 'Normandy pattern', an M43 cap of Army splinter pattern camouflage and an M40 field cap, an Army-issue 'pullover' shirt and short laced combat boots.

ABOVE Anti-tank weapons, from top to bottom: 8.8cm Panzerbuchse 53 (Panzerschreck – 'Tank Terror'), an electronically fired smoothbore weapon with gunner's protective shield in place, with (below) a shaped charge round of about 7.25lb/3kg; Panzerfaust 100m one-round recoilless weapon with simple firing instructions on the charge head, fitted on the reloadable launcher; and an American M1A1 rocket launcher or 'bazooka' for a hollow charge projectile, with (bottom) a training round (introduced in 1942, the bazooka was the weapon from which the Germans developed the Panzerbuchse).

FAR RIGHT A selection of German medical supplies, including a portable field respirator and case (top left) and an oxygen bottle (top right), above which is a first aid kit with metal splints (top, centre). Alongside the field surgery leather saddlebag (right, centre) is a vehicle first aid box (bottom right) and its contents of a limb sling, bandages, ointments, antiseptics, urine test kit, roll of plaster, detoxification kit and cream, and bottle of Rivanol tablets.

RIGHT Each German division had about 60 of these 8cm Granatenwerfer 34 (81mm mortar). The cleaning rod (left) is shown with three types of case for mortar rounds (wicker, metal and a wooden box). At the bottom is the 70cm Entfernungsmesser or coincidence range finder with a mortar sight.

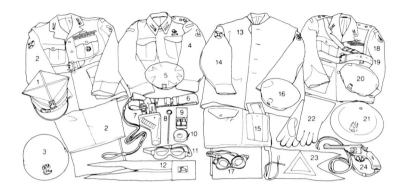

UNIFORMS AND EQUIPMENT OF THE 1ST POLISH ARMOURED DIVISION

1 Polish dress cap

2 Service dress, jacket and trousers of a lieutenant colonel of 10th Polish Dragoons

3 British Royal Armoured Corps steel helmet (Polish insignia)

4 British battle dress with a black epaulet indicative of armoured units and a collar flash that indicates a motorised formation

5 Black beret of armoured units with captain's insignia under the eagle

6 British pattern 1937 with web and holster

7 US Smith and Wesson military and police revolver

8 Brass cleaning rod for the revolver

9 Tin of purification tablets

10 Cleaning compound for web gear

11 British Mk. III goggles

12 Unit designation pennant of 2nd Squadron, 10th Polish Dragoons

13 British jerkin

14 Battle dress blouse

15 Battle dress trousers with field dressing

16 Armoured officer's beret with lieutenant colonel's insignia

17 British issue goggles

18 Service jacket, lieutenant of division engineers

19 Sam Browne belt

20 Armoured officer's beret with lieutenant's insignia

21 British Mk. I helmet with Polish insignia

22 British gauntlets

23 Designation pennant

24 British Webley revolver

RIGHT M1915 Adrian helmets, revolvers and brassard used by the irregular Forces Françaises de l'Intérieur (FFI) and Resistance. The revolvers are a US Smith and Wesson M1917 (left) and a French M1892 (right). The right-hand helmet and the Cross of Lorraine were worn by Leonard Gille, the commanding officer of the Resistance in Caen.

ABOVE Waffen-SS uniforms and equipment, clockwise from top left: camouflage helmet cover; field cap; officer's visor cap with silver cords; officer's M42 field caps; field grey tunic and trousers of an assault gun unit from 2nd SS Panzer Division, with an SS officer's field belt; M42 steel helmet; binoculars (7×50), slide rule, plotting board and compass; camouflage clothing rank insignia (1943); and camouflage smock in plane tree pattern, from 10th 'Frundsberg' SS Panzer Division.

LEFT On the left is a *Luftwaffe* ground combat camouflage smock with M1940 helmet and M1943 *Luftwaffe* field cap. On the right is a *Luftwaffe* service cap with a lightweight summer flying jacket and trousers. The identification manuals (Allied aircraft and armour) are accompanied by a double barrel flare/signal pistol.

ABOVE A selection of *Luftwaffe* qualification badges. Top row first, from the left: ex-flyer's commemorative badge in a case, ground combat badge, parachutist's (*Fallschirmjager*) badge and anti-aircraft artillery (*flak*) award with its original cardboard box; pilot's badge, observer's badge, air gunner/flight engineer's badge with envelope and wireless operator/air gunner's badge with case.

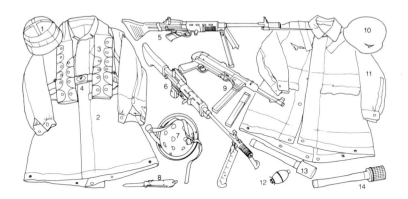

GERMAN AIRBORNE UNIFORMS AND EQUIPMENT

1 *Luftwaffe* paratrooper's helmet with splinter pattern camouflage cover

2 Second pattern *Luftwaffe* camouflage jump smock ('bone bag') with jump fasteners on the lower edge of the smock that turn the skirt of the smock into 'legs'

3 Paratrooper's 100-round bandolier of 7.92mm ammunition for 98k rifle

4 Waist belt and steel buckle

5 M1942 paratrooper rifle 7.92mm calibre, first type

6 FG1942 (*Fallschirmjäger Gewehr*) paratrooper rifle, second type

7 *Luftwaffe* paratrooper's helmet interior view with leather liner and chin strap

8 *Luftwaffe* flight utility knife (gravity blade knife) issued to flight crews and paratroopers

9 MP40 machine pistol with 32-round magazine

10 *Luftwaffe* paratrooper's steel helmet with single *Luftwaffe* insignia decal

11 First pattern grey-green jump smock

12 M1939 hand grenade with suspension ring

13 M1924 stick grenade

14 M1924 stick grenade with fragmentation sleeve attached

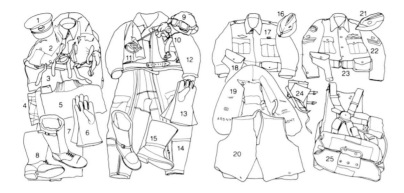

RAF AND ALLIED AIR FORCE UNIFORMS AND EQUIPMENT

1 RAF officer's service cap

2 'Mae West' life jacket

3 RAF battle dress with emergency whistle at the collar

4 Silk escape map

5 Wool turtleneck 'white frock' sweater

6 Leather flying gloves

7 Battle dress trousers

8 Pattern 1943 flying boots – the knife inside could be used by downed aircrew to turn the boots into civilian shoes

9 Leather flying helmet, goggles and earphones

10 Oxygen mask and radio

11 'Mae West' life jacket

12 Sheepskin flying jacket

13 Leather flying gloves

14 Sheepskin 'Irvin' flying trousers

15 Fleece-lined flying boots

16 Norwegian Flying Officer's side cap with national insignia (the wearer of items 16–18 flew in Normandy in August 1944)

17 Battle dress jacket of the Royal Norwegian Air Force – note national insignia

18 Pattern 1937 RAF blue web belt, pistol holster and ammunition pouch

19 'Airvelope' – early pattern life jacket

20 Sheepskin vest worn by a Royal Australian Air Force (RAAF) pilot and signed by members of his No. 453 Squadron

21 Royal Canadian Air Force (RCAF) side cap

22 RCAF battle dress of a Flight Sergeant

23 As item 18

24 Leg desk and map case

25 Type S, Mk. IV parachute

ABOVE The colours of two of the Polish regiments that fought around Falaise as part of the 1st Polish Armoured Division commanded by Major General Stanislaw Maczeck: 24th Lancers (left) and 10th Dragoons (right). After Falaise the dominating heights on Mont Ormel, held onto valiantly by the heavily outnumbered Poles, were described by Montgomery as the 'cork in the bottle'.

BELOW Mementoes of General von Choltitz who commanded the German strongpoints in Paris to surrender. His vehicle pennant, M1913 J.P. Sauer u. Sohn 7.64mm pistol and holster, and his 1889 Prussian Infantry Officer's sword and scabbard.

LEGACY

The visitor to Normandy should visit at least three cemeteries: the German cemetery at La Cambe; a UK Commonwealth War Graves Commission cemetery, of which there are 18; and the Normandy American Cemetery and Memorial at Colleville-sur-Mer.

La Cambe contains the remains of 21,222 soldiers, sailors and airmen who fought for Germany in the Normandy campaign. The majority were killed between 6 June and 20 August 1944 and their ages range from 16 to 72. The cemetery is dominated by a central ossuary housing the remains of 296 men, of whom 207 are unidentified. Many of the interments are in shared graves, reflecting the German tradition of burying 'comrades in arms'. It is a very sombre place, representing the challenge of commemorating those who fell in occupation of foreign soil and is reliant

'With its melancholy rigour it is a graveyard for soldiers not all of whom had chosen either the cause or the fight.'

La Cambe cemetery wall inscription

upon the goodwill of the host nation. Given the fact that many on the German side who fell in 1944 were neither German nor committed Nazis, the inscription (below, left) on the wall outside conveys a powerful message.

For any British national, a visit to a UK Commonwealth War Graves Commission cemetery feels like a local parish churchyard. The cemeteries in Normandy contain over 22,000 UK and Commonwealth servicemen, with Bayeux the largest one of all. They are places to quietly walk, think, contemplate and reflect upon the sacrifices made by a previous generation.

In contrast, the Normandy American Cemetery is, unashamedly, more of a celebration of freedom. It contains 9,387 marked graves and the Garden of the Missing naming 1,557 US servicemen. The focus is very much on the United States' commitment to European Security in a post-1945 Cold War context.

This is important. The lesson of the First World War was that the Allies concept of 'victory' contributed to the conditions in Germany that led to the rise of Nazism. After 1945 the Western Allies made a conscious effort to rebuild the shattered heart of Europe. This also had an element of realpolitik given the growing ideological confrontation with the Soviet Union. The Western allies had not fought one form of tyranny only to see it replaced by another. The legacy of D-Day is the freedom from tyranny that western Europe enjoys to this day; freedom not just from Nazi persecution but also the commitment made in 1944 by the Allied powers to freedom from all oppression.

LEFT Two British veterans at Bayeux War Cemetery to commemorate the 69th anniversary of the D-Day landings on 6 June 2013. The cemetery is the largest in France for Second World War Commonwealth soldiers and 4,648 men lie buried there, mostly casualties of the invasion of Normandy. There are also 466 graves of German soldiers. Opposite the cemetery is the white stone Bayeux Memorial for the 1,800 Commonwealth casualties of Normandy who have no known grave, which reads: 'We, once conquered by William, have now set free the Conqueror's native land.'

For the UK, D-Day signalled the transition to a role subordinate to the United States as that nation assumed the global leadership role. For France, the legacy is still a bitter one, focusing as it does on the question of resistance versus collaboration. Perhaps once France truly assesses its past by commissioning an official history of the war, that process might begin in earnest. For Germany, which it could be argued has come to terms with its past, the legacy is quite simply the ability to talk about that recent history and to commemorate those who fell for their nation, but without celebrating the political system or the cause for which they fell.

All this begs the question, why do we remember? The simple answer is to make sure we do not repeat the mistakes of the past. The sacrifices made by thousands of servicemen and civilians during D-Day for the freedoms that we enjoy to this day is the true legacy of that momentous event.

FURTHER READING

Anyone looking for further information about D-Day, OVERLORD and the Normandy campaign is faced with a range of books and other media. This short essay is very much my personal thoughts on the most useful and accessible sources for those with a general interest in the subject.

In terms of narratives of the campaign then Antony Beevor's *D-Day: The Battle for Normandy* has a judicious blend of comprehensive coverage of the major events but with the focus very much on the human experience of war. This is a powerful combination, and Beevor's is perhaps the best starting point for a campaign overview, from the launching of D-Day to the Liberation of Paris, as well as being a fantastic read. I would add to that Robert Kershaw's *D-Day: Piercing the Atlantic Wall*, which again focuses on the human stories within a chronological narrative, but his book closes following the defeat of the initial German counter-attacks and the fall of Carentan. Seamlessly moving between grand strategy and the tactical and human aspects is Sir Max Hastings' magisterial *Overlord: D-Day and the Battle for Normandy 1944*, which is quite rightly judged a classic text that takes the story up to the closing of the Falaise Gap and the effective end of the Normandy Campaign.

For those who require further details of the actual landings, Ken Ford and Steven J. Zaloga's *Overlord: The Illustrated History of the D-Day Landings* is a good start, including good perspective illustrations of key elements of the landings, which allows the reader to unpick what are often complex and confused tactical situations. Also from Osprey is *The D-Day Companion: Leading historians explore history's greatest amphibious assault*, edited by Jane Penrose, in which I have to declare a vested interest because it includes a number of essays by my former colleagues at the Joint Services Command and Staff College. It is organised thematically, and is a scholarly yet engaging work, picking out key themes and assessing them in some depth. For example, one of the often overlooked elements, the planning of NEPTUNE, is assessed by Andrew Gordon, who is currently writing the first biography of Admiral Bertram Ramsay, which will greatly add to our understanding of Ramsay's career and his role in the planning and conduct of NEPTUNE. One work that does look at NEPTUNE is Chris Yung's *Gators of Neptune: Naval Amphibious Planning for the Normandy Invasion*, which is perhaps a bit too specialist for the general reader but it remains the only volume on the subject, even if it is too North American in its focus.

If the murky subject of espionage has piqued anyone's interest, Ben Macintyre's *Double Cross: The True Story of the D-Day Spies* will certainly be of much use, containing as it does wider information about how the British use of double agents assisted with FORTITUDE and hence the overall success of OVERLORD. Steven J. Zaloga's *D-Day Fortifications in Normandy* provides much detail on the German defences faced by the Allies on 6 June 1944.

A number of volumes present eyewitness accounts, the vital evidence for the work of the historian. Of particular note is Ronald Drez's *Voices of D-Day: The Story of the Allied Invasion, Told by Those Who Were There*, which draws on the University of New Orleans' Eisenhower Center's oral history project launched in 1983 to capture first-hand testimony. It is, naturally, North American in its content, but provides much, readily accessible, source material. Redressing the balance is Roderick Bailey's *Forgotten Voices of D-Day: A Powerful New History of the Normandy Landings in the Words of Those Who Were There*, which draws on material in the Imperial War Museum to provide a wealth of British accounts of the 'Great Crusade'. The D-Day Museum at Portsmouth also has an accessible range of eyewitness accounts on its website: www.ddaymuseum.co.uk/d-day/memories-of-d-day.

For readers planning a trip to Normandy, an invaluable resource is Major and Mrs Holt's *The Definitive Battlefield Guide to the D-Day Normandy Landing Beaches: Sixth Edition with Latitude and Longitude References*. Not only does it contain six potential itineraries for those wishing to construct their own 'battlefield tour', but it is packed with information and first-hand accounts. Anyone travelling to Normandy should have a copy in their rucksack.

In terms of other media, the Normandy episode of Thames TV's epic 1973 series *The World at War* still has much to commend it (as does the entire series). Perhaps most important are the testimonies of eyewitnesses who are allowed to tell their stories within the overall narrative.

Finally, in order to gain some impression of 'what it was like' then *Saving Private Ryan* really must be watched for its accurate, highly visceral and horrific opening half an hour. Charting the arrival of the 2nd US Rangers into the chaotic hell of Dog Green on OMAHA beach, their initial disintegration under heavy German fire and the key role of junior officer leadership in pulling them together, it is an assault on the senses and still leaves one stunned as to the ferocity and randomness of death and survival during the infantry experience of World War Two. In complete contrast is *The Longest Day*, which, while not without its problems, provides some good context; of particular note is the decision-making process and the pressures building on Eisenhower before the final decision was made in the early hours of 5 June 1944 at Southwick House. The HBO TV series *Band of Brothers*, based on the Stephen Ambrose book of the same name, details the story of Easy Company, 506th Parachute Infantry Regiment (PIR), 101st Airborne Division: their training, the drop into Normandy, a heroic assault on the guns at Brecourt led by Lieutenant Richard Winters, and onto Carentan and beyond. Interviews (available in the boxset) with members of Easy Company are both invaluable and extremely moving.

ARTEFACT LOCATIONS

The artefacts featured in this book were photographed from the following collections:

Airborne Museum, St Mère-Eglise 10-11(22), 44(r); Allan D. Cors Collection 98, 99, 110-11; D-Day Museum, Portsmouth 14(r), 15(l), 30, 34, 56(l), 69(l), 75, 94, 113, 127(11); Eisenhower Library and Museum 14(l), 15(r), 20, 26-7(1-12), 76-7; Fistrovich Collection 147; John Frost Historical Newspapers 126-7 (1-10); Henri Levaufre 1, 10-11(21, 23); Joseph McFalls Collection, Newton Sq. PA 57; Memorial Museum, Bayeux 10-11(1-20, 24), 74, 82-3, 86-7, 95, 96-7, 106-7, 108-9, 112, 121, 124-5, 138, 140, 141, 144, 145, 150; Military History Shop, Kennett Sq PA 134(r), 146(l); Milwaukee Public Museum 134(l), 148(1-4); Museum of the Liberation, Paris 3, 31, 153; Musée du Débarquement 68-69; Patton Museum of Cavalry and Armor 5, 136-137, Pegasus Bridge Museum, Bénouville 84, 85, 122, 123; Royal Marines Museum, Portsmouth 56, 120; Russ Pritchard Collection 46-7(17, 18, 20, 21), 70-1(7, 21), 58-9(1-23, 25, 26, 28), 134(headwear), 134(r), 148 (8, 10, 12-14); Sikorski Institute 31, 142-3, 152; Tony Stamatelos Collection 46-7(1-16, 19, 22-30), 54-5, 61, 67, 70-1(1-6, 8-20, 22-6); US Army Ordnance Museum, Aberdeen MD 58-9(24, 27, 29), 72-3, 139; West Point Museum 26-7(13), 44(1), 148(5-7, 9, 11)

INDEX